Not Needing New

ABOUT THE AUTHOR

It took a life-changing event for **Anna Kilpatrick** to realise she needed to turn her life around and find a sustainable way of living. By embracing second-hand fashion, uncovering life hacks that prioritised underconsumption, and finding the joy in what she already had, Anna realised that she loved living with less! After starting her hugely popular Instagram account @not.needing.new to document her journey in 2019, and being featured in money-saving articles for the *Guardian*, *The Times* and more, Anna found her place among the second-hand/slow-fashion community, and now hopes to inspire others to have a sense of happiness and contentment as they willingly, or otherwise, are being faced with less.

Not Needing New

Discover the Joy of Enough

ANNA KILPATRICK

First published in Great Britain in 2026 by Orion Spring,
an imprint of The Orion Publishing Group Ltd
Carmelite House, 50 Victoria Embankment
London EC4Y 0DZ

An Hachette UK Company

The authorised representative in the EEA is
Hachette Ireland, 8 Castlecourt Centre,
Dublin 15, D15 XTP3, Ireland (email: info@hbgi.ie)

1 3 5 7 9 10 8 6 4 2

Copyright © Anna Kilpatrick 2026

The moral right of Anna Kilpatrick to be identified as
the author of this work has been asserted in accordance
with the Copyright, Designs and Patents Act of 1988.

All rights reserved. No part of this publication may be
reproduced, stored in a retrieval system, or transmitted
in any form or by any means, electronic, mechanical,
photocopying, recording, or otherwise, without the
prior permission of both the copyright owner and the
above publisher of this book.

A CIP catalogue record for this book is
available from the British Library.

ISBN (Hardback) 978 1 3987 2634 5
ISBN (Ebook) 978 1 3987 2635 2
ISBN (Audio) 978 1 3987 2637 6

Typeset by Goldust Design
Printed and bound in Great Britain by Clays Ltd, Elcograf S.p.A.

www.orionbooks.co.uk

For my beloved brother-in-law
Brian Melville
1956–2023

I did it, B.B.
I did it.

Contents

Introduction	1

Part One

Chapter 1: What Is Enough?	17
Chapter 2: Finding the Sweet Spot	34
Chapter 3: The Second-Hand Trap	51
Chapter 4: The 'Do-I-Need-It?' Filter	64
Chapter 5: What to Get Rid of and How	86

Part Two

Chapter 6: Fashion v. Style	119
Chapter 7: Health and Beauty	144
Chapter 8: High Days and Holidays	172
Chapter 9: Creating a Home	203
Chapter 10: Parenting with Enough	223

A Final Note	248
Recommended Resources	252
Acknowledgements	254
Notes	257

Introduction

In 2012, with two small children at the start of their primary-school lives, I found myself suddenly alone with the financial responsibility of the household following a painful and completely unexpected end to the normal family life we had been living. The marriage to my university heartthrob faced some difficult shifting sands as the decades paced along and we leant closer into the different visions of life that we were holding. In the depths of this time, miles from extended family, and emotionally lost in giving our all to our teaching careers and to our small children, my husband had a sudden and devastating stroke aged thirty-eight. I found him on the bathroom floor, and nothing was ever the same again.

He survived; he's a brilliant force. But we did not.

We lost our home and the children lost their school places in the school where he was a PE teacher. Thankfully I kept my teaching post, but eventually the kids and I had to find a way to manage on less than half of what we'd had access to before – all in the aftermath of the pain and heartache that a life-changing event had thrown at all of us.

At a pivotal time in my late thirties, I was now faced with a choice: spend my life getting into dangerous debt

INTRODUCTION

trying to maintain the lifestyle we were used to, or accept a new reality and work out what myself and my little family really needed now.

This complete change of life has meant that I've had to learn to live with less for well over a decade, but in recent years I began sharing my lifestyle online through social media. This dovetailed with the world beginning to wake up to the perils of overconsumption – financially, emotionally and environmentally. It now feels incredibly important for us all to reflect on how we buy and acquire *new* things and whether our spending is causing more harm than good. Ultimately, all you or I want is safety and comfort, and in this book I am sharing the steps, the stories, and the mindset shifts that have enabled me to enjoy a fabulously 'rich' and happy family life, despite the numbers on my bank statement or the size of my flat.

From the terrible, fearful early days of believing there was just no way that I could manage to provide enough for us to cope, to the peace and contentment of the later years in my tiny flat with the kids, I've learnt that there is so much to gain when we let go of yearning for more. This is what I hope you will gain from this book.

Not Needing New is a powerful way of looking at life; it's part of a positive movement that's shaping up to be the cultural shift of our time, and I can tell you, as someone who was initially forced to take these steps, that as soon as you commit and start to see the freedom and joy that this mindset brings, you won't want to look back. Escaping the quest for more is a gift.

Just imagine a world where everyone around you knew when they had enough. Everyone had enough food to be

INTRODUCTION

healthy, enough space to feel safe, enough heat to stay comfortable, enough clothing to wear – enough of all they needed and no more. Why would you ever be dissatisfied with your possessions if you had just enough of everything that you needed? It may feel wildly simplistic to envisage such a utopia, but adopting a mindset where you're aware of what is enough for you, and not constantly chasing what lies beyond that, is to start freeing yourself from so much of the stress of modern-day life.

The first half of this decade has been tough on everyone and we're realising that the consumer-fixated way of life that's had us all sleepwalking along the conveyor belt, earning and spending, borrowing and accumulating, is not slowing down. There's been an inescapable period of adjustment for all of us as we face both the economic and environmental consequences of this tempestuous era, the absolute least of which is the inevitable dialling down of our central heating thermostats as energy costs soar and the planet heats up. Inflation, interest rates and surging prices have impacted almost everything, from our heated towel rails to the cost of tomatoes, and we've all had to make some uncomfortable changes.

For lots of people, there is nothing *new* about this need to live more frugally. Twenty-one per cent of people in the UK live in poverty and there are many troubling structural and historic factors that contribute to this statistic. If you would consider yourself to be part of this group, I have no doubt there is a lot I could learn from you on this topic of Not Needing New. I hope you'll take from this book what you need and what is realistic. Please feel free to leave the rest.

INTRODUCTION

For quite a number of us, however, it's the first time that we really are being forced to consider what we *need* as opposed to what we want. This reality is uncomfortable and confronting, but looked at in a different light, it could be the opportunity for a fundamental reassessment of what actually matters.

Despite the constant narrative to achieve more, to push, to grow, to accumulate, to reach further, faster, to maximise and to profit, it's not defeatist or self-limiting to begin to cut back and live with less. This very personal form of embracing underconsumption actually feels really good, but we have to make this true for ourselves by learning to see things in a different way. We can learn what *enough* feels like and we can start to spot when we do not need new.

With my affluent adult lifestyle plunged into unexpected chaos in 2012, the family home had to go. Now I live in a tiny flat with my teenagers, without a bedroom of my own, with no garden, no balcony and a kitchen that's just a corner of my lounge – so rest assured that everything you read in this book claiming you can be happier living with less, is coming from someone who has that life, who is actually doing it, and finding that life is not just manageable, it's actually considerably more enjoyable when it gets simplified down to only the things you need, the things that are enough to bring you real, solid contentment.

Now I want to take a moment here to say that I understand that I am privileged in many ways. I am a white woman with a job and a fantastic support network. I know how rich I am in those ways, and the traumatic turn

INTRODUCTION

of events ultimately made me even more grateful for what I have. I can't presume to know anything about you or the hardships you have to face, but I've felt all the good, bad, fearful and ambivalent emotions on this journey and I hope that by sharing them it will help to smooth some of those bumps and edges for you.

When my two children and I moved into the little flat we call home, one thing that was certainly humbling for me was coming to terms with the fact I no longer had a bedroom. In fact, I just have a shelf to sleep on.

It's a big shelf, as far as shelves go, but an elevated rectangular nook, flimsily separated from the hallway with nothing more soundproof than an IKEA curtain, is now my entire 'bedroom'. It makes me laugh to think that years ago I used to feel fed up that, as an adult, I didn't have my own en-suite bathroom.

My start in life taught me very quickly how to share and how to make the most of everything; as the fifth of fifteen children who were always in second-hand clothes, I saw our parents modelling ordinary everyday frugality right from the start.

Growing up in a house with so many siblings, I had a similar 'bedroom' for a while as a child aged twelve. Although a fair bit bigger, that too was a space on the landing, curtained-off from the rest of the rambling house and constantly filled with the blurred voices of my parents and the drifted television/audio snippets of my older siblings' evenings.

As I accelerate alarmingly through my fifties, I certainly didn't plan on life working out this way, with me sleeping in a smaller personal space than I had as a child in that

INTRODUCTION

wild household stuffed with children; nevertheless, here I am, on my shelf above the hot water cylinder, in the only tiny flat I could afford, in the Not Needing New life I find myself in. Yet, oddly, here I am, in smaller surroundings than I've ever lived in, with less money, less privacy, less stuff than ever, and I am probably the happiest I have ever been as a grown-up.

When I first moved in here and had to start sleeping on the shelf, I was anxious and miserable about only being able to afford such a small space, being up high, so close to the ceiling, so aware of my physical position, mere inches beneath my neighbour's bathroom floor. I can hear everything. We're in a block of flats and I am sandwiched between two single guys, above and below me, which, although good news for the electric heating bills, means that I hear the pings of their bathroom light pulls. I hear the rubbery twist of one or the other of them moving in the bath. I hear the flushes, the taps, the coughs. Which presumably means they can hear me.

At first it made me feel compromised and downhearted, but those feelings have gone. Eight years into living in this flat, and I feel incredibly safe when I hear these tiny human rituals. I know that they are there. Even when I'm alone in this flat, if anything were to happen, I know where there are people who would help me at the drop of a hat. I don't ever feel alone anymore.

That clamber-up bed though – honestly, it's not a sacrifice. Every night up there on that shelf feels like an adventure. It's like the times you built a den made of blankets swagged over chair backs in the front room and begged your parents to let you sleep in there, or the time you got to stay the night in a wonderful old caravan. Every night

INTRODUCTION

feels like it contains a bit of magic from the adventure days of childhood. And adventures make people feel happy.

Back when I 'had it all', the serial malcontent was always creeping in. I felt it. I was convinced that I was missing out and I hadn't quite got enough because I didn't have access to an en-suite like so many of my friends. And now? I've got no bedroom at all, just a shelf.

And it is enough.

It's liberatingly, joyfully, calmly – enough.

I can report, having lived with less for many years, that nearly everything surrounding me now, as I write in my beautiful tiny flat, was found second-hand – either charity-shopped, pulled out of a skip, or dragged back from the council tip. I didn't plan to live like this, but I'm so glad I do. In this book I can't wait to share all of the wisdom I have gained and how you can apply it to your own life to access the joy and contentment that can be found in embracing this lifestyle.

Let me give you an example of Not Needing New in action. Recently, I had a completely wonderful birthday for the grand total of £8 – the whole day. Everything. My teenagers stayed up the night before and secretly decorated the flat while I was asleep with the same cotton-fabric bunting we use for every birthday, along with tiny wildflowers in egg cups, Post-it notes and pretty little things we already own. I asked for a letter instead of a gift and that is what I was given – a precious, funny letter from my children that I can keep for ever. I don't think any chocolate, any bath bombs, any perfume could ever be as special as that. My son had 'earnt' a cake when he worked for a local garden party event, and we got that free cake out of the freezer to

INTRODUCTION

defrost. My boyfriend had pulled an ancient enamel house number from the rubble of a skip on a trip to France and gifted that, a beautiful old blue and white rusted number. The £8 was spent on hiring a secure dog field for an hour so that we could totally relax outside without having to keep an eye on the recalcitrant terrier. We did cartwheels and lay back on the grass watching the neatly timed aeroplanes coming into London Gatwick. A perfect day with less, but actually more! Far more. The connections and the moments that we really need as humans. The things that we are actually seeking when we are spending our money.

Many people who saw the picture of this celebration on social media said that they too would love this kind of simple low-cost day, and yet we are so programmed to default into thinking that the more we spend, the better the occasion will be, the happier it will make us. It doesn't work like this. A clear and brave way forward is by gently letting go of the 'want want want' mentality and realising it was never making us happy. It's the experiences and connections which are golden, not the things, and while this may sound blindingly obvious, from the way that we are living, it's clearly taking a while to sink in.

For twenty-three years I was a teacher; throughout that time I taught hundreds of children, in what will have been many thousands of lessons. This book, however, contains the greatest lessons that I could ever pass on. The real stuff. The stuff that can change your life for ever, for the better. My aim is to help you to really know and to truly feel that Not Needing New is OK, and I can safely say that as soon as you begin to welcome that idea into your life instead of being terrified of it, you will start to appreciate things and experiences in a

INTRODUCTION

totally different way – as if someone gave you the 3D glasses through which to view your own contented future.

This book will help you to do some, or all, of the following:

- Stop aching for more.

- Stop spending money on stuff that only brings a fleeting moment of joy.

- Understand that you already have all the possessions that you need to be happy.

- Reflect on your family values and show you how to model being more content.

- Let go of feeling that you need to keep up with other people.

- Lessen your impact on the environment and reduce waste.

- Recognise the things you really do need.

- Encourage you to let go of things you don't need.

- Make you more aware of living seasonally.

- Prioritise connections over possessions.

- Look at ordinary things in a way which makes you happier.

INTRODUCTION

To truly feel the benefit of this advice, I encourage you to embrace an open mindset and be ready to try flipping the usual 'glass half empty'/'grass is greener over there' narrative that you've been constantly fed through adverts – that narrative that hasn't ever succeeded in making you truly feel baseline happy – and you have to be ready to really work at trying to set a different, stronger narrative inside your head. I will not pretend that reading this book, or ANY book, will suddenly make you happy forever – that is not possible and it's not a natural state to be in anyway. Life will always be a mixture of joy and pain and all the shades between. But I believe you can use a Not Needing New view to help you to develop a foundation of contentment, which makes it so much easier to allow happiness to come inching in, in all the small ways that you may have simply been missing out on in the past.

It's not easy at the beginning, but once you start to see the benefits that enjoying enough will bring (contentment, calmness, freedom, financial stability, enhanced individual style, lack of envy – to name a few), you will not want to turn back.

I was first introduced to the idea that I was in charge of my own happiness, and that I had the power to decide that I had enough to be happy, one wet morning in a tent in Wales with five kids and a new boyfriend. The seven of us were in a fusty four-man tent, having a delicious plastic bowl of cornflakes and UHT milk with added rain, at about 7 a.m. one exhausting morning, midway through the week's holiday 'break'. Horizontal sweeps of precipitation were billowing in from one side and the view from the misted-up see-through flap was showing us that the

INTRODUCTION

day was unlikely to grant anything other than an extensive mission to keep everything dry enough to sleep on, in, wear or eat.

Just as a huge drip of summer disappointment splashed onto the back of my neck and traced a cold path down into my cagoule, I looked sorrowfully at the new boyfriend and said, 'This is awful, do you think we should go home?'. He looked back at me and honestly said, 'Anna, this is life. It's beautiful. This is the best there is. And if you're not enjoying this, you need to have a think about what it is that you want . . .'

I could have punched him in the face.

Except (and I didn't really see it then, at that point) he was absolutely right.

There was an element of choice in that moment. My utter disappointment and misery was not going to change anything around me for the better. It could not clear the clouds, it would not bring the sunshine, it was unable to upgrade the tent into a sumptuous glamping bell tent complete with chandeliers of tea lights and dry sheepskin rugs. It would not turn UHT milk into crushed avocado on sourdough bread with the perfect poached egg. I could whinge all I wanted, the day wasn't listening.

He suggested that I accept things as they were, that I stop kicking out against it and just decide to be happy anyway. After all, we're not entitled to a life of unbridled bliss at every moment; on that day, we had enough, the kids were taking our lead, we had all the bases covered. Learning to be baseline content with how things are, to not expect each moment to unfold perfectly and exactly as you daydreamt it should, to respond to ordinary challenges without extraordinary emotions, to accept what is happening without feeling victimised, becomes a superpower. Learning this from Gus is what allows me to access the many pockets of joy that life is offering all the time.

I can't say that I was instantly transformed in that moment, but it was the start of a realisation that we are not simply passive recipients of happiness, but that we have countless opportunities to see the best in small moments and simple objects. To look for the beauty in a pebble pushed into your hand on the beach, to understand that designer brand names do not make the products fundamentally different or better, to look at everything you already have with fresh eyes, and to take the small-scale tricky situations that we are often in and, yes, decide to be happy anyway.

If you catch yourself looking out of the window in the morning thinking that it's grey and rubbish and the day is going to be a slog and you're tired and everything is crap, then you will, very likely, have a crap day. I know it's hard, but practise looking at the grey day and thinking that a walk at lunchtime will be nice, or that you're grateful for your thick warm socks. If you practise deliberately looking for the things that are wonderful, you will get better and better at seeing them and at feeling the real contentment that comes with that. Even when it's a bit of a test, if you have what you need, if you have enough, you can decide to be happy anyway.

The individual actions that I am going to bundle up here for you may not all be uniquely new to you, but it's the process of bringing it all together as a positive lifestyle change and really giving it a darn good go, which will make the shift, bring you the permanent dopamine lift, and allow that gentle happiness to come creeping in in a way that constant shopping has never, and will never be, able to.

I wish I could gather you all up and tell you face to face, over a coffee, about all of the ways that life has actually improved since stepping away from the lure of having shiny new everythings; writing this book has been the best way that I can think of to help you to get to this place of feeling totally fine, too.

Let's get started!

Part One

CHAPTER 1

What Is Enough?

The *Cambridge Dictionary* definition of 'enough' reads: 'as much as is necessary; in the amount or to the degree needed'.[1] To me, this sounds incredibly vague and unhelpful. To understand how much is *enough*, we actually need to find out how much is *necessary* and for each and every one of us, that is going to look completely different.

When I first had to think about what was necessary for me and my children on an average day, I was able to boil it down very simply to food, water, a roof over our heads, clothes and beds. However, it quickly became clear that beyond these basics, each of our day-to-day needs were very specific and needed to be met in order for us to enjoy our lives.

By tapping into my own value system, and listening to my kids, we started to work out what amount of stuff was necessary for us to feel like we had *enough* to feel safe and secure, without stretching ourselves.

Throughout this book I am going to provide prompts for you to engage with, either by thinking them through in your head, or if you're so inclined, writing in the spaces provided or on a separate notepad. Each exercise will encourage you to start interrogating some of these ideas for yourself and thinking about how you might incorporate them into your own life.

In this first exercise, I want us to imagine everything we need on an average day. On this day there is absolutely nothing more that you *need*, and in this scenario, nothing more that you *want*. In order to visualise an existence as zen as that, I want you to stop reading and spend a few minutes thinking about what that would look like for you. I don't want you to play 'billionaires' here; it's not about what you would do if you could have everything you wanted – it's what simple and basic things make you feel safe, in routine and able to enjoy each phase of the day.

Think about a typical day from beginning to end. What bedding do you need to have slept in to wake up feeling well rested? What breakfast fills you up and gives you energy until lunch? Which shoes do you always choose because they're the most comfortable? And what about the 'non-stuff' moments that keep you feeling content? Do you need to walk, swim, or stretch to feel your best? Do you find doing the crossword is important? Or being able to sing in the shower?

Task: Simple Things I Need to Feel Good

Once you have the image in your mind, I want you to note it down either in bullet points or perhaps draw little pictures to show all of the things that create the foundation of a great day *for you*. The small things which make you feel like life is *good*.

For me that would include my morning coffee, some-

WHAT IS ENOUGH?

thing I look forward to each night as I head to bed. A bar of soap with a beautiful fragrance. A dog walk in the local woodland. A fresh pillowcase to snuggle down with. Gone are the yearnings for symbols of success: the en-suites, the new suits, beauty treatments, restaurant experiences. It has all gently breathed back inwards to become a small and manageable type of perfection.

Evening

_____
_____
_____
_____

Waking

_____
_____
_____
_____

Afternoon

Morning

_____
_____
_____
_____

_____
_____
_____
_____

Now you've completed the exercise, how does it make you feel to look at these items? Do you think that a day that only includes these simple items might feel like having 'enough'?

It's interesting that despite being aware of the simplicity of many of the items and habits that bring us the most consistent joy, we can't stop there. Our hopes are so often based around the idea of gaining more stuff, different stuff, new stuff and gaining more space to put that stuff in; changing the very environments where we already know that comfort lies. What we rarely notice is that we have favourites of everything. A favourite pair of jeans that don't dig in, a favourite mug that feels just right to drink out of, a favourite pair of shoes that go with everything and a favourite pen that is so satisfying to write with. All the other stuff that sits in drawers and cupboards is exactly that – *stuff. Clutter. Unnecessary.*

All those items do is give you the illusion of abundance and options, but in this book I hope to show you that abundance and possibility are mindsets, and no number of possessions is going to make you feel safe if you can't build that safety within yourself.

This is at the heart of distinguishing what is enough. Seeing the difference between what you need and what you want; stripping things right back to the basics can become a mindset that you begin to really enjoy, taking pride in the sheer simplicity of what you actually do need, as opposed to the never-ending onslaught of the new material offerings you are told to want.

This pattern of accumulation and future yearnings is so engrained in us as normal, that we just never question it – it's growth, right? But it can't be a *positive* kind of growth if we're missing out on chances to experience how wonderful a more simple life can be, and how much more happiness we can encounter from ordinary little moments when we train ourselves to recognise them.

Paradoxically, the more we aim to gain a sense of self via identity consumerism (i.e. buying things from the brands with labels that we use to tell the world what our values are), the further away we seem to get from feeling connected to anything. There's a niggling sense of shame that comes creeping in when we start to consider how much money and time we have handed over in the quest to make ourselves something different, something that appears 'better', more acceptable. I kid you not – as you head towards the final decades of your life, you will begin to ask yourself why you ever allowed so much stuff to distract you from the simple joys that run like golden threads through your best days and really help you to feel grounded and connected.

It's an interesting exercise to think about all the things that we have packed into our homes to create ease and comfort, and then offset them against all the objects we need to keep ourselves active and healthy. I totally get that half an hour with great music at a spin class may be more enjoyable than hauling your laundry to the municipal washboards and mangling your bedsheets through manually operated metal rollers, but can you see that when we remove work, we need to add work back in somewhere else? We become convinced that we need to buy into the latest fitness accessories to help us to keep fit and well, when in truth, so much can be done with less. Almost everything we want to do in life has already been done for hundreds of thousands of years in a way that's quite simple and won't require masses of new stuff. It's the 'serial malcontent' that creeps in, doing its best to make you believe that there's a new thing you can buy that can solve your issue (in this case, keeping you active) instead of thinking that you can build ordinary access to movement into your daily life and sometimes your fitness 'problem' won't even be there. When we look at the things we're drawn to buy through this lens, it starts to become clear how manipulated we are by the hype around stuff. How many new kitchens are putting in the 'instant boiling water tap' when we've had kettles doing that job perfectly well for hundreds of years?

COMPARISON

In life, it's so easy to fall into a pattern of wanting to surround yourself with the items that help you to fit in and to replicate the lifestyles that you see all around you in magazines, on television programmes or on social media. Usually, the images being displayed are part of clever campaigns to sell us something, so they need to make us want what they show. They display people with above-average incomes, living lives that are not really relatable for most of us. Glossy magazines fill their lifestyle pages with photographs of perfect kitchens, lounges with artisan handwoven cushions and reclaimed vintage herringbone wood-block flooring; objects placed effortlessly on mantelpieces with intentionally crumpled linen curtains letting through the muted sunbeams of the second home in rural Puglia. It becomes a desire-blueprint for our own lives and we feel that we must try to mirror it somehow, to interpret it in the best way that we can to make our nests look like those magazine nests that we dream of. We become locked into this habit of trying to accumulate the items that we think we need, having being fed these items from print and screens, mostly through paid editorial spaces.

The buyers in retail spaces then latch onto the trend, and fill the shelves of our regular shopping and browsing haunts with mass-produced versions of things that look like the things that we've all seen in the fashionable spaces, and we feel even more drawn to the accepted style of the moment. We like what we recognise. Just like listening to songs on the radio, the ones we're used to are the ones that feel comfortable and the ones we get excited about hearing. When we're consistently shown that there's a 'best' style, or some 'must-have' looks out there, and we start to see them showing up over and over again, it's easy to fall in love with the aesthetic enough to begin to subconsciously reflect it in your own home.

Then, for more pressure, add in the 'Diderot Effect'. An identified psychological phenomenon, this is the name given to the reaction following a new purchase whereby the buyer then sees all manner of additional purchases around the primary one, which would also now appear to be necessary, and therefore a spiral of buying and overconsumption occurs. For example, you buy a new kitchen table, and then think that the old chairs need to be changed, which leads you to spot a coordinating sideboard, which makes you think that some pottery would look good on display, but then you agree that you ought to have better lighting to show it off . . .

We do the same thing with clothes and make-up and cars and gadgets; the idea that there is a better version, an upgrade we can make, pervades every single aspect of our daily lives. No sooner have we spent money on the item that was meant to make everything so much better, there will be something to go with it that will begin to gnaw away at our psyche. Our relationships, our transport, our parenting, our leisure – everything is being suggested to us in terms of 'You will be a happier person if you have this', yet we all steadily begin to realise that this simply isn't true.

Sometimes, through unconscious comparison, we put ourselves in a position that makes us feel that if we were to stay still and enjoy the everyday things that we have, we would somehow be failing to create the life that we 'should' be living. We unwittingly slip into 'serial malcontent', where we never feel fully satisfied and the euphoria of the new purchase burns out with such alarming speed that we're already focusing ahead on the next acquisition before the packaging of our most recent purchase has even got as far as the recycling bin.

I'm telling you now, we can put an end to this spiral. We can start to ground ourselves in a mindset of 'enough' by remembering how much truth there is in the saying, 'Comparison is the thief of joy'; indeed, we are often perfectly happy with our lot until we see what someone else has. And seeing what we each have is such a big part of our lives now, with billions of social media windows into the front rooms, wardrobes, kitchens and holidays of those we love as well as those we have never even met. We are confronted with visions of beautiful, stylish new things being used by people just like us, with instant and irresistible links to click and buy them. We are fooled into believing that this is how other people's houses look, how they dress and what they drive. We start to think that what we have is lesser and needs an upgrade. We fall into the comparison trap and we become the principal drivers of our own malcontent; it's very, very likely that no one else is paying any attention to the things you start to imagine that you are lacking.

Despite the constant fear that my children will be shamed by the fact that they have, without doubt, the smallest, least 'impressive-looking' housing of all their mates, there are always teenagers here. I come home from work straight into a room filled with chatting teens making potato waffles in the toaster. They don't see spaces in the same way. They are all positive and encouraging and they seem to like being here. I guess the Wi-Fi password being available has probably helped enormously, but I urge you to remember, if you are feeling that your home doesn't compete with your friend's, your child's friend's, your boss's or your in-law's, remember that people do not come into your house and measure it up in the same way that your anxious eye travels over the walls in your doubting moments.

People remember the welcome, the fun and the warmth way longer, and way more readily than they will ever recall the square footage of your living room or what make your fridge was. The things that you will do inside your home remain exactly the same no matter what 'league' you might place your bricks and mortar in; you sleep, you eat, you wash, you relax – I promise you that the fundamental building blocks of your day-to-day existence will not be magically transformed by a move either up or down that housing ladder, and they certainly won't be changed by a different-coloured sofa or another duvet cover. We all do the same basic things in our homes, no matter the price tags attached.

People are generally happy to take the path of least resistance, the easier path, and will accept the version of yourself that you present to them. If you are beaming out 'apologetic cringe', and you're hanging your head down and trying to shuffle about hiding the version of yourself that you think that they think might not be enough, then you're telling other people what to think about you. They will take that as the picture because it's what you are offering. If you are able to 'own your space' as the saying goes, to be truthful and warm and unbothered by what you have, or don't have, then that is the picture that others will accept.

I struggled with this feeling that I hadn't done well enough for a very long time. I knew that out of almost all of my old uni friends, I have probably ended up as the least 'successful' in terms of career, finances, marriage longevity and property ownership. I used to go to see my friends and carry this fear with me; I had a terrible, negative opinion of myself that made me want to curl up and hide away instead of facing the situations that I was mistakenly reading as competitive.

Let me tell you, it's likely that you are the only one even thinking about all this. People who love you want to see *you*, they want to be with *you*, not the car or the house that you don't own.

WHAT IS ENOUGH?

It really is grounding and comforting to live in the truth: to accept what you have without allowing yourself to be squeezed into financially difficult situations in an attempt to keep up with others. The more that you start to believe that you have all the things that you need, the less you will even think about comparisons between other people you know. You each have enough, you each are safe; you are all in the same situation really.

Understanding what makes us truly happy in life is a life-long journey, and it changes as we age and gain experience; however, building a strong set of values that you can commit to and find an anchor in will help you to navigate that path. Knowing what makes *you* happy, not anyone else, will stop you from living in that state of comparison, and start living authentically as yourself.

Look back at the simple daily rituals that you added to the wheel for your own keys to finding what enough is for you; there you will see the things that you value more significantly than others. Identifying and establishing these values is your personal key to finding contentment with less. If you have been able to pinpoint some of these fundamental contentment blocks, you're already well on your way to enjoying a happier life with enough.

My core values are family, freedom and community.

I can trace these core values through all of my happiest memories. All of them involve being with the people I love, being free to do things at my own pace and being together, sharing a common purpose or goal.

Task: I Was Happiest When . . .

In the next task we complete together, I want you to think back to your happiest times. Take a moment to think about a happy time now. You can use the prompt:

I was happiest when . . .

What can you remember about the settings of these times? What makes these memories special? Is there a common thread running through the good memories? Can you identify it? Write a series of short statements for yourself starting with 'I was happiest when . . .'. For me, it could look like:

- I was happiest when *I was camping with my siblings.*

- I was happiest when *I was chatting in the staff room at break.*

- I was happiest when *I knew my teenagers were safely home in bed after their adventures.*

- I was happiest when *we had picnics in the back of the van.*

_____

_____

_____

_____

_____

WHAT IS ENOUGH?

_____

My hunch is that you will see a picture emerging where the happiest times were about the people, the places, the more simple pleasures in life. Hold onto the awareness that those connections are the parts of your life that bring you joy and hold value.

It's very unlikely that 'stuff' is what holds the real keys to your heart and your happiness. Working on recognising these experiences and connections as the most precious parts of living, and becoming more aware of what is enough by making a mental note of the times that you feel truly content, will help you to edit out the times when you're tempted to buy items to try to recreate the feelings. Spending money can bring you very short-term spikes of happiness, but if you're interested in a far steadier contentment, try to find the opportunities to recreate and build into your calendar some of the rituals or practices that have given the greatest feelings of joy; the groups, the environments, the relationships.

Look at your 'happiest' statements. What could you be doing more of to access the feeling of pure happiness more often?

And consider the new things that you want to buy. Ask yourself not only how they will look, but what are they adding to the values that you want to promote for yourself?

Be honest with yourself here – what's on your mind to buy next, right now? New trainers? Shine-enhancing shampoo? Sleek little coffee pod machine? Which products are calling to you? The ones that will propel you into the better life that you have in your imagination, the life that you think you will be happier in . . .

Task: Be Brave and Name Them!

When you've thought about the things that you're currently considering, take a moment to jot three of those items down on the bag on the next page. Then, go back to the wheel you created at the beginning of the chapter and the list you just wrote of the times you have been happiest. Can you make any connections between the things that you think you want right now, and the practices and moments that bring you the greatest sense of contentment?

For instance, if you listed a walk as one of your most grounding and essential moments of the day, and you're thinking about buying headphones so that you can walk

WHAT IS ENOUGH?

and listen to the podcasts you enjoy, then that's a purchase that you already know aligns well with your personal values and is worth considering. On the other hand, trends, which we become aware of and may temporarily intoxicate us, where there are no links to our daily contentment values, can be ignored – these are not the things that are going to support our long-term happiness and may likely become the things that weigh us down with consumer guilt and the clutter of the unused at home.

    Another way to decide if an item you're considering is something you should actually buy, is to very intentionally visualise your life, and how different it will, or will not be, when the new item has been bought. You need to ask yourself if you already have anything that serves the same, or a very similar purpose? Be exact here – try to nail down

specifically what will be different in your life with the newer thing? What *real-life* changes will it bring?
For example:

- There's a new type of raincoat I have seen other people wearing – I want it, but I already have a raincoat.

- This one is just a more fashionable colour or brand and that's why I want it.

- It won't really change my life beyond that.

Or:

- There's a new type of raincoat I've seen other people wearing – I want it, but I already have a raincoat.

- However, this one is much longer and will keep me drier when I have to walk the dog in the rain.

- This one will make a discernible difference to my real daily life.

It's a really good exercise – each time you start to think about buying something, properly imagine your life with the new thing in it. Try to clearly visualise everything else being just as it is, and as it still will be, but that one new thing you want has been added. Try to think with absolute honesty about exactly how different your life will be after

WHAT IS ENOUGH?

getting it, and how much of an impact this one thing will have on your normal life, to your baseline level of happiness and ease. Usually you can let the craving just drift off, safe in the knowledge that the glossy promise of what it'll bring will be quite far from the reality of how little life will actually change.

If this exercise doesn't always stop you from buying, don't panic, there's no need to feel bad about the times that you do decide to go for it and invest in a new item. If you succeed once out of every four or five times and you manage to curtail the impulse buying that would not have served you anyway, then that's a massive achievement and you will have reduced your consumption of unnecessary new stuff by 20–25 per cent just from your own simple thought intervention. Well done!

Hopefully at this point you are starting to build a picture of what *enough* might look like for you. What values you want to hold onto and what you might be ready to let go of. Through the rest of the book, we will keep exploring these questions and start tackling some of the more practical actions you can take to start living a life of contentment with less.

CHAPTER 2

Finding the Sweet Spot

This isn't a book about living like a monk or a minimalist. This is a book about finding the sweet spot between being overwhelmed by unnecessary stuff that's only going to bog you down and cost you more than you have, and managing a life so frugal that you struggle to find the joy. Together we are going to find that blissful sweet spot which, I can assure you, is completely within your reach.

We have to work on seeing through that brilliant myth we've been presented with for our whole lives; yes, it's true that new things are often gorgeous to look at and we long to be in those perfect scenes dreamt up by the ad executives who know exactly what will pull at our heartstrings, increase our pulses and wriggle into our psyches, but it's also true that spotting this manipulation and being resolute about what you actually need to be a happy human, will make you feel permanently empowered. Let me tell you, it's a truly good feeling: the bliss of a calm mind and the feeling of having enough.

THE COST OF OVERCONSUMPTION

Just as with food, when we consume too much of anything it can leave us feeling regretful. Have you ever experienced a time when you've eaten too much and felt that physical discomfort? When you wish you hadn't had that final forkful and you're actually suffering because you simply took too much? You can't sleep or rest comfortably for feeling bloated and nauseous – hold onto the memory of what that was like. We will come back to it.

There are some obvious costs to overconsumption of non-food things too; it may not affect our bodies in the same immediate way, but the impacts of overindulgence upon our physical environment, which in turn impact upon our mental well-being, are also important to identify. Below, I am going to cover some of the symptoms I have experienced that might be relevant to you too.

Guilt about the Environment

In this day and age, it's impossible to claim that you're unaware of the global impact of consuming and buying too much. We know about the piles of waste textiles in deserts that can be seen from space, we've seen forest annihilation, massive habitat loss, carbon emissions rising, and river systems poisoned with toxic 'forever chemicals'. We live in a supply-and-demand economy meaning that every time we send a message to a big company that we want more of something, business will respond and manufacturing kicks up another gear. And who benefits from this? Not us and definitely not the workers creating the products. We know this, and it doesn't feel OK.

I have, in the past, bought things knowing full well that they are not really needed, that they are just for one tiny moment in life, or that I was shopping to make myself feel better after a tough day at work, or a relationship low. These purchases haven't been good; the guilty feeling sticks in the memory, whispers to me when I see what I bought and ruins the joy of having the item anyway.

Sir David Attenborough has been trying his hardest to warn us for years, series after stunningly shot series, that unless we do something drastic and immediate, we are going to have to continue to witness the ongoing destruction of the planet as it buckles under our punishing demands. The environmental crisis the world is facing is already demanding that we relinquish our unnatural expectation of having to have all the things all the time. Raspberries in December, pizza to our door at midnight within fifteen minutes of tapping an app, fresh seafood available regardless of our inland locations, super cylinders of piping hot water surged into our power showers morning and night – we are each using up way too much and it has to change. In wondering what on earth is happening to Earth, we find ourselves having to examine our own role in fuelling inequality and injustice through our rampant consumerism.

But unbearably, even with footage of lethal sweatshop factories collapsing, crushing workers to death, with clips of wildfires ravaging through streets and homes, floods sweeping cars and structures downhill like toys, nothing that has ever been said by Sir David, by Greta Thunberg, or by any of the world's finest orators, has ever been enough to change our collective addiction to having all the things, all the time.

'It won't matter this one time . . .' we tell ourselves, 'just one more little Amazon order won't make a difference.'

Until now. 'Just one more' is making a difference. It's impacting us directly. Our cavalier use of world resources in conjunction with the economic squeeze we're experiencing, is finally waking us up to the impact of having too much, and the idea of 'underconsumption' has actually become a trending concept to those of us who have had lives of such excess.

Personal Debt

Globally, times have been very tricky, both economically and emotionally. So many of us are feeling squeezed as a result of spiralling prices and stagnating wage growth. The economic optimism of the nineties has crumbled into far leaner days where the majority of us are readjusting to a more frugal way of life in order to just keep going. This can leave us feeling miserable and without joy. It's hard to see how things will get better any time soon.

Add to this picture the relentless bombardment of product advertising on social media via devices in our hands that reach out to us during every waking moment to promise us so much, and you have a recipe for malcontent – less money to spend, making us feel pinched and miserable, adverts promising to alleviate that mood, spending your money to grasp the promise, and then the item naturally not managing to deliver all it promised, so more misery, more spending – and it goes on, leaving us feeling trapped and unable to keep up.

According to a mid-2020s government briefing paper, 46 per cent of UK adults had used some form of consumer credit within any given year.[1] Credit card debt was over £70 billion in the UK in 2024 – working out at over £2,524 per household[2] – with many low-income homes over-indebted and only able to pay the interest on the amounts they have borrowed. The relative ease of borrowing on cards and the rise of BNPL (Buy Now Pay Later) options like Klarna have made it very normal to live beyond the reach of one's income and to build up financial troubles for the future. I remember a time when I was automatically offered a £10,000 credit limit on my card. Ten thousand pounds – for a single parent on an average salary. It was only the absolute fortune of being able to make my second-hand lifestyle and shelf-dwelling flat work for us that enabled me to avoid having to head into that hot water. The ease with which credit is offered is directly proportional to the toil of trying to escape the trap of increasing debt.

Clutter

You only need to watch one episode of the disarmingly delightful Stacey Solomon in her television programme *Sort Your Life Out* to see how we manage to unintentionally accumulate huge amounts of clutter. Stacey and her team help one family per episode by removing every single item they have in their home and laying it all out on the floor of a vast warehouse for sorting. Imagine finding out that you had 437 pairs of shoes, 188 spoons and 39 phone chargers. Almost everyone I know has an issue with clutter, and it gets worse every year.

Let's face it, property and space is not cheap. Maybe you're building storage units and using up loft space, spare rooms, garden offices, bulky IKEA boxes, cramming your garage just to store things that you will barely ever look at again, let alone use daily? You will have to clean them, or clean around them, move them if you're going anywhere new, insure them if you fear losing or breaking them, and basically handle the emotional burden of ownership. There is a sort of 'bloating' to face as your home fills with everything you're buying, and perhaps even a sense of nausea when you have to look at the financial implications of accumulating all of these things.

Clutter is known to affect our anxiety levels, our focus, decision making and task avoidance, and even our sleep. Higher levels of cortisol, a stress hormone, have been identified in people who live with a cluttered environment. Our brains enjoy a level of organisation and routine, where we can have 'space' for higher-level processing as the basic mechanics of daily tasks are simplified through order and calm. If we are surrounded with constant visual and physical reminders of disorganisation and chaos, this creates a sort of cognitive overload and reduces our capacity to deal with other stresses.

There is a reason that estate agents want to photograph properties with almost clinically uncluttered surfaces; we instinctively feel drawn to spaces where we will be free to move, free to think, free to enjoy being without feeling suffocated by objects crammed into every conceivable space.

Constant Cleaning and Tidying

The bigger your space, and the more stuff you fill it with, the more there will be to clean. More surfaces to wipe, more flooring to vacuum, more clothes to launder, more bathrooms to sanitise, more lawn to mow. Greater amounts of any of the things that we desire heralds a greater curation of responsibility and is the primary reason that people often describe the letting go and downsizing phases of their lives as liberating. It may seem a slightly intense example, but I will admit that for the past seven years of living in the flat with no outside areas, having been forced to live family life without a garden or balcony to escape to, the children and I have spent so much more time enjoying the benefit of shared community spaces, and these are places that we pay for indirectly through taxation but ones that we are not obliged to maintain ourselves with endless mowing, sowing or weeding. My flat is small and I can get my own cleaning done in short blasts of activity leaving me free to spend my non-office time outside in calming nature, or choosing to do something else that makes me feel good. I don't need to pay a cleaner as it's small and quick to manage, and really importantly, I don't feel overwhelmed by the constant obligatory tasks associated with running a home. So many of my friends have much more to manage, in terms of numbers of rooms, the amount of possessions and just basic square meterage of outside spaces to handle. Having less may feel difficult to reframe as a benefit to begin with, but there are certainly advantages to time and freedom in choosing to live smaller.

Self-Judgement and Judgement of Others

I think a lot of us feel deep down that there is something not quite right about having too much. Let's think about some of the language around it and what emotional reactions the words create – hoarding, becoming avaricious, gluttony, hoggishness, mercenary, spoilt. We feel slightly ashamed of ourselves for overspending and stashing things away; we may even start to hide how much we have. Overconsumption can trigger feelings of negative self-worth and may affect our friendships when we begin to judge other people for the amounts they are accumulating too. Watching others buying more and more can provoke jealousy, feelings of insecurity at being 'left behind', scorn, or even pity, as we wonder what emptiness is trying to be filled.

Over the years of having my social media account, I've heard from hundreds of people who have struggled with negative feelings of self-worth related to shopping; a sense of shame at not feeling able to have resisted buying more and more when they knew that there was nothing left that they needed. Sometimes these behaviours lead to stress within family relationships as others become aware of the build-up of products coming into the home and the financial implications involved.

Feeling Out of Control

Compulsive Buying Disorder (CBD) in its most amplified state is a recognised form of addictive behaviour. It comes when the desire to shop feels uncontrollable and only the purchase of a new item can offer temporary relief from stress, anxiety or boredom. The act of shopping becomes so key to feeling anything positive that the person will continue to spend despite all the difficult consequences, the financial struggles and associated relationship stresses. It's often experienced by people who are suffering with low self-esteem due to other factors in life and is a way of escaping the harder realities that they are having to deal with, but ultimately creates a more distressing situation.

CBD in extreme cases can be completely overwhelming to manage and there are addiction services that can offer support. If you don't have CBD, you can still experience a disassociated feeling upon the delivery of a huge online order and you are left wondering which version of yourself even placed the order in the first place? What were you thinking? Who were you buying all of these things for? Who were you trying to impress? By finding ways to delay spending and avoid impulse purchases, we can save ourselves the discomfort of feeling disconnected from ourselves and our values.

'Spoiling' Your Children

Perhaps this is a little controversial to add here since everyone has very different ideas about what spoiling a child means. In this case, I simply mean encouraging the same 'more, more, more' attitude that you might see in yourself, in your children; perhaps using lots of things to show love rather than sharing the values we covered in the last chapter.

But the concept of 'spoiling' is not only to do with the overindulgence of material items given to the child – toys, sweets, extravagant parties, designer clothes – it may also be a lack of tasks or responsibilities being assigned to them, as well as a parental reluctance to ever say no to a request for fear of upsetting them. Having a house full of barely touched toys not only negatively impacts the parental bank account and the sense of space and calm, but it fosters an expectation in the child to have all the things, all the time – a mindset that we are trying to dismantle for the benefit of ourselves and our environment.

With small children particularly, having less leaves room for the most wonderful play opportunities (more on this later) and opens up the creative possibilities of more imaginative games. And with all children raised in a loving environment, where the ability to wait and to delay instant gratification is built into the rhythm of the home, a particular strength and resilience is nurtured.

Lack of Boundaries in Relationships

Spoiling children isn't the only way that boundaries in relationships can be affected by too great a lean into consumerism. The giving of gifts in any relationship has potential to be a truly lovely way to signal commitment, to strengthen memories and show deep appreciation of one person to another; however, it can also be misused as a tool. It can be used as a form of control or manipulation and can be abused as a replacement for decent behaviour and respect. Being fully equal and fulfilled in a partnership leaves no aching need for gifts as outward signs of attachment and commitment, and can open up the possibility for tiny things to feel like enough.

In friendships too, issues with boundaries and spending can create problems. If a friend is insistent that you join them in booking expensive holidays, extravagant restaurant trips, high ticket-priced concerts, and they have ways of making you feel guilty if you say that you're unable to, then you need to work on understanding your own clear boundaries and feeling absolutely empowered to communicate them and stick to them. True friends will understand and support you in this, potentially deepening your bond through trust and honesty.

THE POWER OF KNOWING YOUR OWN MIND

When you begin to find the sweet spot of enough, you will be able to happily step away from the exhausting clutter and distraction of more, and with your leadership on this, you can welcome in a different vibe to your home – a capsule wardrobe, an uncluttered house, a strong bond with fewer, loved items; it will be quicker to get ready when you need to, and you will see a more developed personal style emerging. You won't be a follower of trends – you'll be your own person.

What's wonderful about the route we're going to take together through this book is that you'll clearly see that you're able to move away from the negatives we have explored and enjoy a really contented lifestyle without these feelings. You get to decide when enough is enough, and prevent yourself from suffering the impacts of too much. Once you start to embrace the Not Needing New lifestyle, you'll enjoy so many benefits, such as an increased sense of calm, less anxiety through clutter, free time away from maintaining the home, a healthier bank balance and reduced debt, children who are learning how to manage delayed gratification, improved relationship boundaries and friendships where the truth is accepted and respected.

WHAT TO DO WHEN YOU FEEL PRESSURED BEYOND YOUR SWEET SPOT

There are often real emotional anchors involved in our consumer habits and it can feel deeply upsetting to be challenged, either from external pressures, like moving in with someone and being asked to reduce your belongings, or even from your own realisation that you have too much and things will need to change. It's not an easy thing to dismantle something that has felt comforting for so long.

It's very important to note that when people have experienced a time in their life, particularly in early childhood, when their family unit had to manage with less than enough, it's a totally natural human response to protect yourself from the negative memories associated with that hardship by accumulating a safety net of more than enough around you, or through shopping as a way to feel empowered and to access experiences that were denied to you in earlier years.

It can also feel difficult to handle situations that occur when you're the friend or family member who has less than all the others in the group. When you are the one with the smallest home, the income that isn't enough to manage buying rounds of drinks or to pick up the meals tab, to buy tickets to shows and hotel rooms, it feels hard. It's also sometimes hard for your children to recognise that you have the 'worst' car, the oldest clothes, the fewest gadgets, the least exotic holiday photos. How do you navigate the issue of pride when you live with less than the others?

We *think* we know what others are thinking and we then

start to act as though that is the truth. You may think that it's embarrassing to have a 24-year-old car with a tape cassette deck and windy windows when your old friends are in huge 4x4 Volvos and Porsches with Bluetooth screens, but you have no idea what they are actually thinking. They might love your way of life. They might wish they had kept their old wheels, they might tell their kids to look out for you coming up the street and they might feel incredible joy at the sight of you. They may wish they hadn't taken the loan out for their car, and probably more likely, they *might not have given it a single thought.*

So, be honest about your situation. Telling the truth has never tripped me up. If there is a girls' weekend planned and you cannot afford it this time, then you must say that. You need to allow other people to be able to do the things that they can do without feeling resentment, and you need to free yourself from feeling like you have to keep up if you can't. Wish them a brilliant time, and say you'll join them for something else. People will respect this and you will find that there will still be times when you can be part of it all, and times when you will be leading it all.

And what about any truly unkind comments you receive? How should you react to the suggestion that you are being dirty by wearing and using preloved things? How do you deal with criticism when people accuse you of not caring because you didn't buy the biggest birthday gift or manage to afford the hundreds of pounds for the hen party in Ibiza? Well, with regard to second-hand things, I like to remind people that there are in fact many, many incidences, even in the most luxurious lifestyles, where things are reused over and over again. Every person who stays in the penthouse suite of the finest hotel in the land will be sleeping on sheets that have been used and laundered. The glasses, forks and napkins used in Michelin-starred restaurants will have been in the mouths of the previous diners, washed and returned for service. We all use things that are not entirely virgin and that is the way it should be. With regard to your decisions about spending your money and making your own choices about what you will budget for, you have to develop a strong sense of self-worth; strong enough to withstand criticism and strong enough to realise that you are absolutely allowed your reasons and you don't have to argue the point with anyone. When you treat others with kindness and compassion and are brave enough to share your truth, you can hold your head up and know that you deserve the same respect back.

You're only ever going to be able to change the way that *you* view things. You won't be able to control other people's thoughts and opinions, so this is the key area that you have to focus your attention on, on your feelings and reactions rather than anyone else's. Let's think about a time where you were unable to put yourself first and you were pushed into saying yes to something that you knew you couldn't afford.

Task: Reframe Shame

Can you recall a time when external pressure from friends or family was enough to coerce you into spending money on something that you didn't feel right about?

Spend a few minutes going back over what happened and remembering the feeling that you had. Trust yourself and the feelings that came up for you. Now try to imagine the same situation but saying what you really felt. What could you have said?

Can you replay the scene and imagine yourself placing clear boundaries around what you were able to manage? Picture yourself calmly sharing what you wanted to say.

Are you now able to imagine a different ending? One where you were able to respectfully untangle yourself from other people's demands in order to protect what was right for you and your household? What would that look like?

ARE YOU SATISFIED?

We started this chapter wanting to discover where the sweet spot lies, and wondering how we can easily get to it. The answer isn't the same for everyone and it will feel both easy and difficult for the changing situations of each person. It might be incredibly easy for you to know where your sweet spot lies with holidays, for example – you have a reasonable budget and you stick to it; you see the things you want to see and you are left neither yearning for something 'better' or dealing with debt. But the same person may find it much harder to work out the sweet spot with shoes and bags. They may have a real love for these things and have developed part of their personality around being known for their enormous collection of footwear and accessories; for that person and that aspect of life, finding the sweet spot will be much more of a challenge. We need to understand that satisfaction – arriving at a point of contentment where you know your needs have been met – comes from within and is not an external experience that we must ask other people to validate for us. We each know what our values are, we thought about them in Chapter 1 when we traced them back to our happiest memories. If we can connect with these values again and use them to help shape our goals and our limits, we will become much better at understanding where our sweet spot is, and feel able to notice it and enjoy it.

I have realised this in moments where I have walked away from another 'bargain' in a second-hand shop, when I have managed to ground myself in the knowledge that I don't need another new plate for the house, but I do need the train fare for a trip next week. Managing to empower myself with the means to get that train instead of burdening myself with stuff I don't need and creating a dent in my account is actually a great feeling and one that makes me feel like I'm doing well, making the choices that I believe in and being true to myself and my values.

Understanding that satisfaction comes from personal limits and goals that we set, casting aside outside opinions and connecting with the values we set in Chapter 1. What does it mean to find our own sweet spot?

Knowing when you've reached this sweet point, the

point of satiation, is hugely empowering and will give you the willpower to step away from temporary temptations that pop up and make you feel like you need another new thing. You will be able to avoid the uncomfortable feeling of overdoing it, the feeling we tried to recall at the start of this chapter. You will remember, with the sureness of your whole physical body, how perfectly balanced it feels to have, to take, to own – enough.

CHAPTER 3

The Second-Hand Trap

OK! You're on your way. You've decided to stop doing so much shopping, you may have cancelled some subscriptions and you're determined to break your mini-addiction to buying new stuff. You have thought about your core values, you care about sustainability and you have discovered the thrill of the charity shop!

However, I'm going to help you try to avoid a very common mistake now. It's really easy to get revved up about letting go of the need for new to begin to see through the marketing that has guided you into so many transactions in the past, and to step straight into the warm and wonderful world of the second-hand community.

Now, hugely importantly, there is such a lot that is right about the second-hand community and I am a massive fan of exploring all the ways to use what we already have, but the second-hand trap is real and no matter how wholesome it might feel, it's not going to help those of us reformed shopaholics.

What can happen is that people transfer their reliance on shopping *new* for their dopamine hit, to shopping *second-hand*. In this scenario, no habits have been addressed. Sure, it's a 'better' shopping habit, but it's still a shopping habit and worse – the thrill of a bargain can be even more addictive. In getting to the heart of Not Needing New and welcoming in the joy that you can experience when you hit the sweet spot of enough, you have to consider whether you're visiting charity shops, scrolling through Vinted, eBaying, etc. because you need something, or if you're still overconsuming for the thrill of the 'new', and still defining yourself by the material possessions that you surround yourself with.

I'm talking from experience here. I fell into it myself.

My entire Royal Doulton bathroom suite – the lavatory, the bath, and the basin – cost me the grand total of £20.

I bought it on eBay in 2017 and incredibly (in my adoring eyes) no one else placed a bid. So, I won! I 'won' – have you ever thought about the language that eBay uses when you are simply buying something, and what it does to you to have it framed as a 'win' rather than a purchase? Anyway, the reason no one else placed a bid?

It's pink.

Absolutely gorgeous pale pink. The pale pink of the insides of shells and the tiny fingernails of new babies. I love it so much. When I bought my tired little third-floor flat, an unconventional place with two front doors on two different corridors instead of a fire escape, a flat so far from the lifestyle aesthetic that it had been previously rejected as 'too grim' by a friend's student son, I began the process of ripping it apart to make it my home. It was slightly intoxicating; I realised that I could, without negotiation, fill my space with whatever I wanted. Granted, I didn't have any money and was struggling to support two children on my less-than-average solo wage, but I had eBay, the tip shop, charity shops, Facebook community bits and bobs groups, and every skip I walked past was worth a peek inside.

I managed to get everything I wanted pretty quickly and really cheaply. At the tip, I got chairs, plates, lampshades, rugs, little tables, taps, shower fittings and a dresser. I started to feel the thrill of accumulating; the lure of the bargain. I got enough for myself and for the children, and enough for any guests who might suddenly come round and want to have dinner with us, but I didn't stop there. I kept returning to the tip and to the Facebook pages in order to see what else was being offered, what other bargains there were to be had, and I was doing the same thing with clothes. I became almost obsessed about finding new outfits in charity shops and would spend a massive amount of my free time looking through second-hand places to source more outfits than I could ever possibly have needed.

GETTING TO THE ROOT OF THE ISSUE

Although this was great training in many ways, for it taught me how to look for fantastic quality clothing and showed me how to live entirely without buying brand-new items for well over a decade, what I needed to recognise, and what I hope you will begin to recognise yourself, is that in replacing your first-hand shopping habit with a second-hand shopping habit, you are not addressing your levels of overconsumption and it's overconsumption that's driving the entire global business economy to keep making more and more and more, and to keep driving down costs to maximise profits.

All consumption has *some* effect, even second-hand, and it began to feel more important to start enjoying what I already owned rather than filling my home with bags of preloved hauls. I realised that real change would only come when I started addressing the greater issue of individual consumption overload, and began to feel both the freedom, and the personal and social benefit, that came from exploring my own point of enough.

The only way that we can begin to dismantle the highly destructive consumer situation that we are in, is to recognise that we need less and to reduce the amount that we are each using. It's our responsibility, in the relative safety of a more developed economy, to do this. And we need to try doing this without over-celebrating our underconsumption either, because we're not actually 'under' consuming if we're simply using all of the toothpaste that's in a tube, or we've cut down from having nine wool jumpers to having six; we are still consuming much more energy and resources than the vast majority of the world's population. It's not truly underconsumption; it's simply consuming a bit less than before.

Consuming what is enough is where we need to get to, but that's very hard, and so far from what we have become used to.

Buying second-hand is an absolutely awesome way to make the best use of the things that have already been produced and it should be promoted and celebrated, but when we are buying anything at all, it's important to check in with the level of need we are facing. We need to ask if we are justifying a new purchase because it's second-hand and therefore excused from being counted as 'proper shopping'? Remembering that there is such a thing as the 'Second-Hand Trap' is a good way to help you to assess how you may still be burdening yourself with way more than needed. Replacing any shopping habit with a pre-loved and 'sustainable' version of the shopping habit isn't going to help you to experience the relief of getting closer to enough.

I would also ask you to revisit the symptoms of over-consuming that we covered in the last chapter: guilt, clutter, debt . . . they all still apply here, which is why we need to get honest about our habits.

We need to ask ourselves what's at the heart of this, what it really is that's driving us to keep buying, to keep the accumulation habit going, even managing to shift it into the second-hand sector. There's something going on, some kind of hole that needs to be filled.

I say this as someone who has spent over a decade finding and filling that hole. At some point in the early survival months after my life collapsed, a friend of mine, who is both a great artist and a psychotherapist, offered me a low-income discount on her weekly therapeutic women's art journalling course. The very thought of going to a group like that had me recoiling in horror. There was no way I wanted to sit and weep with women using their own menstrual blood as drawing ink, because that was what my imagination told me it would be like. I created every excuse not to attend, but she kept on encouraging me. I was too tired to keep thinking up reasons not to go based upon the scenes that my imagination was conjuring up so I did eventually go, and in actual fact, it was amazing.

Of the many tasks that she asked me to do, one was

to create a list of all the things that I truly loved, without anyone telling me that I ought to love them. The things that sparked joy for me. She had a theory that some of us lose our egos when we get into relationships, and again, if we have children, and in doing so, we forget what we used to like. We forget our personalities and passions.

It's probably easy to see how, coming from such a large family, I adopted a strategy of mostly doing what other people wanted me to do, in order to make life easier. Believe me, you can't really have tantrums, stamp your feet, demand a pony, expect constant lifts to activities, have someone to decorate fairy cakes with, blow dry your hair or even know what your favourite cereal is, when there's more than eight other children in the same house. People are busy. Just washing the clothes is a full-time job. Being a chameleon is a good strategy.

Yet remaining a chameleon in an adult long-term relationship is a very poor strategy and so many of us do just this; we adopt a sidekick mentality and start to like the things that our partners like, forgetting what joys were once ours.

Making that list of what I liked under my own steam was the first time that I had even realised that I have gone along with whatever other people have wanted for years, letting them have the lead. I soaked up other people's taste, quirks, ideologies and routines. I could barely remember what I stood for and cared about. I let myself be second in all the major decisions in my own life. Making that list would be the start of seeing that I was a valid individual and that I had my own interests that I could nurture.

Making your own list is, fascinatingly, a rather difficult

thing to do and I really encourage you to give it a go. It will help you to see what you need around you in order to feel more fulfilled and generally happier. Try to peel away the layers of influence so that you can remember and rediscover what really lights you up. It can't be the band you loved when you were a teenager, if you only got into that band because you wanted your brother's cool mates to like you. It can't be wild swimming if you were taken to the sea by your friend who raved about how much she loved it and you reluctantly went along because all those wild swimmers seemed so damn grounded and fearless and you just wanted to be part of that gang. What you have to try to do is free yourself from all forms of persuasion that you have been subject to, and ascertain which of your likes are totally *your* likes.

Creating this list of the things that you love without the influence of anyone else in your life is a very good thing to do. It informs you about where to place your future focus in terms of your time and your money, in order to gain real happiness, rather than the cuckoo happiness that you found in someone else's nest. It helps you to be able to stop turning to glossy magazines to show you what you should be buying. You can be the buyer, the stylist, the editor of your own life; you will begin to see what makes your heart sing, and when you work that into your life, you can let go of needing to match what everyone else is doing.

Task: Make That List

Get a journal out and doodle it all down. Put yourself in the middle. Go right back and try to recall your childhood interests. What were you drawn to? What places, music, foods, colours, characters? What did you leave behind that you could pick up again?

THE SECOND-HAND TRAP

I still have my list in the art journal I made. We had to work in silence after the initial circle of conversation. I found that almost unbearable at the start. I like to fill in all awkward spaces with something. But being silent means you have to sit with yourself and listen to what comes up, so go somewhere silent for a while and see what comes up for you.

My list, still in the journal that I have kept, is what came up for me and it's written in the tiny writing of someone not quite sure that these are good enough things. It tells me that I like (and consider how useful this is going to be for my future): 'Trampolines, Slow-Worms, Lizards, Clear Thai Soup, Little Lights, Noticing People's Teeth, Convertible Cars, Soap'.

It's funny, though, how many elements of contentment in my tiny new life feature these things, quite by accident I thought, but maybe, when you put your real loves around you, the things that resonate deeply with you, you are able to switch off from the unabated pressure to keep getting more stuff, new stuff, and you can begin to feel content with so much less. It's almost as if the unfillable hole, which you're trying to pack with your shopping patterns of the past, is magically fixed by finding the right materials.

All of these things slowly and steadily have filled my cup to overflowing. I no longer have a lingering void calling to be filled by *new stuff* because my life is filled with more connection, activity and excitement than it ever was before. I have explored lots of different avenues and there are a few I would suggest you should try if you're finding it hard to kick the buying habit. We're looking to crowd it out with all the good, fun stuff!

Pick Up a New Hobby

Engaging your creative side in any way can boost your mood and give you a sense of accomplishment and pride that overrides a need to have something new. Engaging in a hobby that you love can not only feel relaxing, but can actually reduce blood pressure and counteract depression. Cooking could be a fabulous way to cultivate a hobby where you might need to buy a few new spices, but they're going to get put to excellent use and nourish your precious body bringing a deep satisfaction. Along my Not Needing New journey, I bought myself a small guitar and have fulfilled a lifetime dream to be able to play enough chords to have a campfire songbook. If I have down time, instead of scrolling through retail sites, I scroll for songs and chords and add another one to my notebook.

Embrace a More Active Lifestyle

Looking after your health can be a brilliant way to spend less time and money on stuff you don't need. Adding in any sort of movement to your day is not only a distraction from looking at online shopping, or scrolling past influencers showing you their PR hauls, but it will improve your health and longevity, something far more desirable than having another new handbag or dressing gown. There are literally millions of free online fitness and movement challenges on YouTube, but for me the big change was getting a dog as soon as I left full-time teaching; there is now another living creature in the flat who depends entirely on me to facilitate all of his exercise and enjoyment. I have no choice but to get out and walk, whatever the weather, whatever the time of day. I have worked out that with the mileage we do together each day, I could have walked to Brazil. Being out and being so aware of the seasons has been a very calming and grounding influence and almost certainly has helped me to manage life with less.

Reach Out to Community

Fostering a sense of your own belonging and connection with others who live around you through getting involved in community action will give you a strong sense of purpose and meaning, and stimulates the production of dopamine which, as we know, leads to positive feelings (this time, without shopping!). There is a myriad of opportunities here, from joining a book club, becoming a school governor, volunteering in a charity shop or community fridge project, coaching sports teams, singing with a choir, getting involved with local politics or wildlife preservation – there are so many ways to find connection and purpose that will fill your cup as you support others. Win–win!

Therapy and Self-Care

A wonderful way to start to unpick some of the reasons why you may have struggled to say no to spending is starting therapy. Doing this sort of guided deep-dive into your habits is transformative and may help you to be kinder to yourself moving forwards. Although this is often an expensive undertaking, investing in yourself this way can be something that frees you from years and years of negative behaviour patterns. Always look for a therapist with accreditation from a professional body, like the BACP (British Association for Counselling and Psychotherapy) and look into practitioners who may have a sliding scale of fees for lower income clients, or even the opportunity to work with supervised trainee therapists who have a much-reduced fee. If face-to-face sessions are not for you, there are many titles in the self-improvement sections of libraries and bookshops that may call to you and support you in understanding and changing your habits and patterns.

SO HOW DO WE KNOW WE ARE FREE OF THE TRAP?

Well, we can never be totally free of buying stuff and this doesn't have to be our aim. It will always be a part of life to seek what's needed and to bring in the things we need to make life comfortable. We are simply aiming to make more sustainable choices and reduce the negative impact of our shopping ways. If you have made a switch and are shopping second-hand, using all the new access points available with apps like Vinted and Depop, then you should be very proud of the change you have made and yes, you do deserve a pat on the back!

Having said this, it's important to recognise that there is an easy trap to fall into where we simply slide over to preloved and continue to consume just as much as before, if not more, under the comforting guise of sustainability by default due to the fact that it's not new. You will start to really feel free of the trap when you know that the things you're choosing to spend your money on are the things that truly sing to you, the things that align with your values, the things that are manageable for your budget and are not

THE SECOND-HAND TRAP

being bought to impress anyone other than you. You will not be buying to fill any void, ache, or feeling of being lesser-than. You will know that buying this thing is the start of a great relationship with an object that holds real worth for you. That's when you know you're content, and free.

CHAPTER 4

The 'Do-I-Need-It?' Filter

Right, so we know some of the ideas around enough, some of the ways to differentiate between need and want, and some of the ways to check in with ourselves about satiation and the experience of knowing that we have what we need in the present, but even with all this self-knowledge, there will still be times when we're drawn to something new in a powerful way.

This is not some kind of personality failure that means you're a bad person; it's just a real and pretty unavoidable consequence of growing up in a culture that focuses so much on the celebration of the accumulation of things.

Think back through every step in your life and you will be able to see that when you had been good, unwell, welcomed in, sent away, successful, or when you had simply existed for a certain amount of time, you were probably rewarded with a 'thing'. We have family traditions which are inextricably linked with gift-giving, the most obvious of which start at the very beginning of our lives: the giving and receiving of presents for birthdays and for major religious and cultural festivals. We celebrate milestones and changes of all kinds with presents; we start collections as

THE 'DO-I-NEED-IT?' FILTER

children: stickers, rubbers, teddies, fan merch. We get persuaded to wear new things to keep up with style and we are rewarded with approving attention when we do; our phone companies want us to upgrade and they box these gadgets as if they were gifts too – all around we are programmed with the message that more stuff is the reward: if we do well, we will receive. More is what we want, and more is what we deserve. It's a greater influence than just the effect that adverts have – it's a deeper capitalist social conditioning. However, it's still true that adverts are going to try their best to lure you in.

Billions of dollars go into advertising; in fact, as I write this, the year's ad spend projections look set to hit $1 trillion globally, for the first time, with a huge annual increase of over 10 per cent[1] attributed mainly to new forms of AI marketing. Don't think that this isn't impacting you. You will never be far from an advert telling you that a magical product exists that will improve your life, and consequentially, that you deserve it.

So that we can try to see ourselves within this landscape and navigate the obstacles here, we need to drill down into advertising, and become more aware of what it does to us and why. We need to understand a very basic history of modern advertising.

For most of the nineteenth century, it was the case that adverts were written in long copy; there would be full sentences in newspapers or magazines, alongside a single-colour line drawing, asserting the powers of a product. People were engaged in the reading, they had time to consider the claims and jot down the name and address, perhaps with a distinctive logo for them to recognise also drawn in the space. The adverts focused on the specific features of a product, and of the product alone; it was not placed within a desirable 'lifestyle'.

Fast-forward to the early twentieth century and there was something of a revolution in the ad world. An Austrian-American called Edward Bernays was changing the way that advertising worked, for ever. Bernays was the nephew of Sigmund Freud, the founder of psychoanalysis, and Bernays himself was fascinated by psychology and by what could be manipulated through the power of suggestion. A journalist in his early career, after the United States entered the First World War, Bernays was hired by the Committee of Public Information (CPI) to help President Woodrow Wilson deal with the immense military U-turn he had made by sending troops overseas and into the conflict. Bernays created a highly successful campaign for the home audience which depicted the German army as an encroaching beast-like enemy, and a direct threat to Americans who had previously tended to view themselves as somewhat removed from the fighting, thousands of miles away across the vast ocean. Such was the power of his spin that thousands signed up to the army following the campaign and public opinion swung in support of the nation's involvement in the war.

After the war, Bernays realised that the propaganda that he had orchestrated had worked so well that his theories about the manipulation of the masses could become commercial gold dust for big business. What his time at the CPI taught him, was that his belief that the population had a herd mentality was justified, and if he could find the right emotional touch points, he could probably get people to buy into almost anything.

THE 'DO-I-NEED-IT?' FILTER

He soon found companies who wanted to put his 'magic' to the test. One of the most well-documented of his ad campaigns involves Lucky Strike cigarettes in the thirties. At the time smoking was superbly popular among men, but few women were buying cigarettes and openly smoking as, for women, smoking in public was seen as a sign of promiscuity and low social morals. The American Tobacco Company, who owned the Lucky Strike brand, were conscious that they were losing out on half of the potential market share of adults if this accepted view was allowed to continue. They had stagnating sales, were not close to being the tobacco market leaders, and had green and red branding that was, in its colour palette, considered to be too unfashionable and a clash with the stylish, desired clothes of the epoch, but they were unable to invest the huge sum it would require to completely change all of their packaging and branding.

Hiring Bernays to get women buying was pivotal to their subsequent profit revolution. He worked firstly on campaigns where instead of looking at the actual superiority of the physical cigarette that the women might buy, he worked on imagery and taglines that would reinforce the strong social message of the time that 'thinness' was highly desirable and that their cigarettes would curb the desire to eat – smoking them would be a 'healthier' alternative than turning to sugary snacks when hungry. He commissioned images extolling the beauty of super-slim women who are fully *in control* and able to suppress the desire to eat by reaching for a cigarette and therefore achieving the required aesthetic and bagging the desirable men, a far cry from the shameful promiscuity formerly associated with smoking. It worked – sales to women rocketed.

A second campaign for the same brand aimed to scoop up the more independent and free-thinking female market by manipulating the idea that the cigarettes and the act of smoking them were akin to holding 'Torches of Freedom', for if men were allowed to smoke in public, why should women feel ashamed to do so?

Bernays managed to both attack this stigma and to address the problem that the company had with unfashionable packaging, by persuading highly influential women of the day to attend a charitable Green Ball where an unnamed sponsor (our cigarette company) would be making a large donation to a charity. He arranged the event to take place at the Waldorf Astoria Hotel in New York and sent press releases to the prestigious fashion houses explaining that green fabrics would be needed, as well-known guests would be seeking suitable outfits to attend. He instructed the photographers to capture the guests walking in while smoking Lucky Strike, and wearing their fabulous new outfits all styled in the same colours as the branding of the cigarettes.[2]

He really started the entire pattern, which we now take for granted, of moving the spotlight away from the individual product and what it offers, to the wider world around the product and what that might offer instead. You are not buying just the cigarette, you are buying access to the 'thinness' goal, which will lead you to a rich and handsome suitor, and access to a glamorous life. You are not buying a cigarette, you are buying a 'Torch of Freedom', which defines you as a woman of worth and value in your own right; people will have to hear your voice and take you seriously.

THE 'DO-I-NEED-IT?' FILTER

This tactic of selling you 'the dream', rather than just the 'thing', is what we now almost expect from good adverts. Take the global outdoor brand Patagonia. They don't show you an ad with their latest fleece jacket pictured, they show you a massive panoramic sweep of snow-capped mountains and a tiny dot of a human in the fleece because the scene setting, the 'dream setting', is a more powerful emotional tool in the task to persuade you to part with your money. The product has secondary importance to the social or cultural message that is being portrayed; you are being promised something MUCH bigger that you can't, in fact, be promised at all. Consider the number of times that you watch a new ad and try to guess what product it will actually be for, because you're often not sure until the end.

There is emotional manipulation going on here and we need to be able to spot it. Bernays argued that humans are all weak-minded and will act as a herd, which sounds harsh, but feels quite true when we look at how quickly trends come and go. He considered advertising to be simply the 'engineering of consent' to twist and trick us into believing that we need something, because he maintained that we will inevitably be drawn to follow *something* as a group, and in getting in first with consumer distractions, it may well be saving us from more radically dangerous allegiances.

Bernays lays down the blueprint for the 'lifestyle' ads, then along comes another American maverick, Bill Bernbach. His creative innovation in the fifties and sixties was to blend super-short copywriting with quirky visuals to create not only standout campaigns that stayed with you long after you had looked away, but ones that could be consumed and understood within a second. This meant that adverts were now free to break loose from the shackles of their papers and appear in spaces where people had less time and were simply passing by. Now ads were becoming bold and big, clever and fast, and we became unable to escape them in the infrastructure of our lives. There is a bit of a myth that in the developed Western world, we are exposed to tens of thousands of ads a day; recent independent research by an ad industry journal shows it's actually much closer to 100,[3] taking scrolling ads, inbox ads, physical marketing materials in public spaces, billboards and television into consideration, but even so, it's a constant barrage to the extent that we have developed a significant 'blindness' and don't even see all of it as advertising due to the subtle ways that marketing has shifted into our everyday realm and is able to promise us far, far more than the thing we are being told to buy.

How can this be remedied by us? What can we do to pull ourselves out of Bernays' herd and take real control of the things we want? It all comes back to Bernays' strategy of working with our psychology. It comes back to understanding the difference between need and want, and recognising the danger zone when you are fooling yourself into the idea that one product is capable of transforming your life. We need to give ourselves grace when this happens; after all, we're at the receiving end of a behemoth industry pumping billions of pounds into our manipulation, but we possess the skills to see this and we can free ourselves from the power it has over our choices, our finances and our time.

THE 'DO-I-NEED-IT?' FILTER

The task in this chapter is laid out in a simple flowchart. If you can, take your time with this one. Think carefully about your responses and dig deep; try to be as honest as possible. It can be difficult to do this when we are already aware of what 'the model answer' would look like and we are programmed to want to please or to want 'top marks', but if you can, be real about the products that have caught your eye recently and are making you want to spend.

Task: Behind the Desire

As you begin this task, I want you to think, really honestly, about something that is currently on your mind that you would like to own. Something that you know is a not an absolute necessity, but that nonetheless has crept into your mind's wishful shopping basket and entered that halfway hinterland of being an 'almost bought' item; it's only going to take one slightly rubbish day, or two decent glasses of wine and it'll be on the way to your house.

In this task I am trying to encourage you to identify any of the bigger outcomes or feelings that you are seeking through buying the new thing. If you already have something like it, what's going to be different about this one?

Take yourself through this little flowchart on the next page:

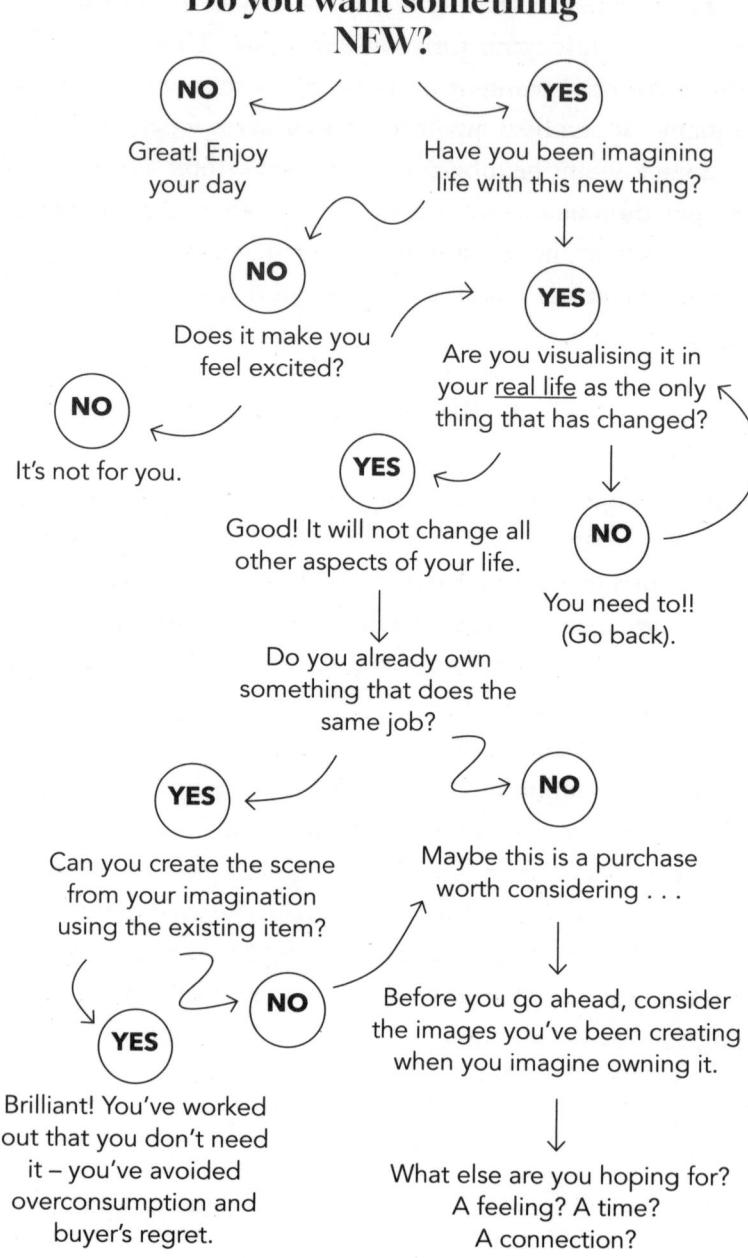

THE 'DO-I-NEED-IT?' FILTER

Have a think about whether there may be a greater need that you can identify for yourself that is sitting behind the desire to buy. It might be that you are spending a lot of money on small things from your daydream, when holding back might be a better way for you to have the means to get directly to what your heart desires. For instance, if you spend money every week on hair accessories, hair styling products, home colour kits and fancy conditioners to have a look that you like, while telling yourself that you could never afford to get a professional haircut in a salon, it might be that you are holding yourself back from getting the thing you really want. Is there anything that you can do to step towards the bigger purchase or goal that you actually crave?

In some cases, the things that we are trying to buy for ourselves may just be too difficult to get to through saving up, or by sacrificing smaller purchases for. Sometimes we buy to fill the ache of grief, the pain of a broken relationship or the rejection of a parent. These things are huge and can't be solved with the forgoing of an occasional online splurge or trip into town and I do not wish to either insult those who are in this situation, or suggest that they remove a strategy that may well be the thing that helps them to get through the darkest of times. Just getting some insight into understanding what you might be subconsciously searching for beyond the product can be helpful though, even if you still need to look after yourself in this way.

* * *

Let's go back to adverts and the emotional power they have. When you are there, at the point of buying something that you have been daydreaming about for a while, you will have imagined a world where you already have it. You will have recreated your own version of an advert in your mind, with you as the principal character, loving life with your new item. I have definitely done this hundreds of times. You see the dress, you admire the dress. You see it shown on other fabulous people living fabulous lives. You look it up online, perfect elegance; you hunt it down. In your mind you're in the dress, walking along a dappled-sunshiney lane running your hand through long meadow flowers. In your mind you are walking into the pub garden with your friends, everyone is happy and smiling back at you, the dress is giving you access to a life of joy! You are running through the plaza in a European city on a romantic break, you see yourself in sepia cine film, slowed down to a hair swish and the floating of the fabric, pigeons scattering ahead as you turn and laugh at your lover over your shoulder. The dress is so great. It's perfect for all these scenes! You will be so happy in all of these scenes with this dress!

But wait – none of these scenes are your life. You're actually going to the supermarket and walking the dog.

You need to stop creating the ad.

What you have to do is pull the product into your real world rather than let yourself fall into the trap of the high budget made-up world that the product is being shown in. You need to get really good at imagining for yourself. You have to visualise the dress in your house right now with no other changes, hanging on your rail. Visualise it

THE 'DO-I-NEED-IT?' FILTER

with your shoes and coats, and only with those. Visualise it in the places that you will actually be going to (probably not a Viennese castle, or a Guatemalan lakeside); basically, imagine that you *already have it*. *Visualise it right now in your home.*

It's just there, hanging about, being a dress. Made of material. Hanging.

How has your life changed? This is the hard part because it's not so fun. It's sobering. You imagine the real-life impact of the addition of the item and it's so much less than the fantasy would have you believe. It's such a good, robust exercise to get into the habit of though, and you will begin to see that certain things you want *will* survive the process, and you will know that they actually will bring real change to your real life. These are the things that you need! Perhaps not 'need' as in survival-level need, but they are the things you need to do the things you want and to go to the places you want to go. Other things will not survive the process and these are the things that you will not miss. They were not required in your life and would have simply become the wardrobe-fillers and the attic fodder.

We don't just do this with clothes and shoes, we tend to do the same with the new bedding that we want, the curtains, the BBQ, the vase – we build a vision of a life with the new item in it, but as well as the item we will also re-paint the entire backdrop in a more pleasing depiction. We are complicit in our own deception.

What we can find out about ourselves from the adverts we create in our minds, is however, a rather illuminating and useful thing. Instead of berating ourselves and seeing it as purely a negative way that we are being manipulated, there is something in our daydreams, even if we know and understand that we don't always need the thing that started the dream off. If you consider what you have been putting into those dreams, you might be able to see some of the actual things that your heart is desiring, the real keys to your contentment.

Take my running through the plaza example, as cringy as it is, that is actually one of the standard images I have when I like a garment and my head is momentarily turned. I see myself wearing the thing and I'm usually in the Praça de Comércio in Lisbon, heading to the steps of the central statue even though I live in a village in a forest in Sussex. It's one of my favourite places ever. I have realised that this placing of myself in this particular setting when I daydream about clothes, is not about the dress, the coat, the shoes – it can never be realised through the buying of those things. It's just about wanting to be back in Portugal, about wanting to feel young again, about wanting to capture those butterfly days of first dates in my twenties and there isn't a blouse or shoe in the world that will bring that back.

What I can do though, is work on spending my limited money and energy trying to get myself into that fantasy I have created, not via the dress from the shop, but by realising that what I actually wanted was something else. I wanted to be in a new place, I wanted to feel really loved, I wanted to feel excited. I could do a much better job of achieving this if I decided to put my energy directly into making those emotions a reality. I know that my access to these feelings has very little to do with what new clothes I have just bought. If anything, spending my limited funds on buying the dress that I'm imagining being there and wearing, is going to push me further from the ability to pay for a trip to be there.

The truth is, I could go back there and actually take myself to the square, take my partner, run across the stone vastness and live it for real; after all, it's what my heart desires, and I could do it in any of the clothes I already own. I do not need a new dress to make this happen, if this is truly what I long for. The dress is not the key here.

Beginning to use this discipline of asking yourself what you are trying to gain when you are buying something will be a very useful way of separating out and avoiding loads of impulse buys that will not serve you in the way that you had hoped.

It's important not to become completely unrealistic about want and need, and not to berate ourselves for the fantasy, or even the reality, of buying more than the basics. We are part of the hugely complex societies that we live in, with all the millions of conditioning experiences, and we tend to operate within the general norms that are set by the billions of feet who have trod these paths before us.

Of course, there will be things that we want that are beyond the 'basic physiological need', the very lowest, most foundational level of the famous triangular psychology graphic devised by Abraham Maslow in his paper, 'A Theory of Human Motivation' in 1943.[4] This now-famous graphic shows an equilateral triangle divided into five equal horizontal bands, with the widest at the bottom and the narrowest at the top. The differing widths, as the triangle tapers to the top, indicate the degree to which each band is essential for healthy human life. The bands, from bottom to top, are: Physiological Needs (air, water, food, warmth, etc.);

Safety Needs (health, security, employment, etc.); Love and Belonging (family, community, intimacy, etc.); Esteem (self-respect, status, recognition, belief in self); and Self-Actualisation (creativity, spirituality, becoming the best version of self).

Maslow describes how we have levels of need beyond the ones that merely serve to keep our fleshy corpus alive and breathing. They may not take up as much bandwidth in our lives as the most obvious needs we must attend to, but with Maslow's argument, there is also a need to be safe, to feel belonging and love, to feel pride in accomplishments and to feel that you are meeting your creative potential. Without all of these aspects of what it means to be human with human needs, we will not have the innate strength of the triangle, standing firmly on that broad base and reaching up as high as it can go.

This conflates to offer a huge spectrum of opportunities for things that you will need, and yes, you are allowed to need them.

There will be certain things that will enable you to be a cook, a painter, a parent, a mathematician, and it's all right to recognise which of these things fall into your personal band of need, the things that you need to ensure that you are having your needs met. If there are tools, and by this I mean the items that enable access to an activity which keeps you feeling sane, then you can honestly include them in the things that you need. You will know, in your heart of hearts, when you push that beyond need and into excess, when you are surrounded by multiples of things that serve the same purpose, when you have yet to open things you have ordered and you're still bringing new things in, and if you have already reached this level, then you will have a really good starting place for some thinning out of the too much that you are holding onto. The next chapter on 'What to Get Rid of and How' will help you to get started.

So, still at the point of buying something new, let's go back to the main question and see if we can apply a cognitive filter – do I really need it?

USING THE FILTER IN REAL LIFE

WAIT, Visualise!

I'm going to give you an easy to remember initialism (WAIT) to help you decide when to buy and when to walk away. It starts with the whole word – WAIT – and ends with you visualising your real life with the product you're dreaming of.

So firstly, **WAIT** – the immediate tactic we're going to use here is quite simply, delay. Slow down and take a pause. Wait. Our desires change frequently because we are exposed to such rapidly rotating ideas about what's 'in'; companies can't let us buy once and then enjoy that product until it's no longer useable because they're under constant pressure to increase profits. Your personal information is gold, your email address is gold – companies want to have you on the list so that you can be sent the latest styling images of their newest items directly, so that you are tempted to buy again. (It can be really helpful to use the unsubscribe button at the end of marketing emails that you are still getting – it will help you to avoid the temptation that is being served up to you daily. You can still remain loyal to the brands you enjoy when you need something, but if you do unsubscribe to the marketing, especially from massive brands, you will find that you are not going to be so frequently dissatisfied with what you already have simply because you won't be thinking about what else there is out there.) There's a song from the nineties that keeps replaying in my mind when I know I'm in the temptation danger-zone – the band James had the hit song 'Sit Down', with the lyrics, 'If I hadn't seen such riches, I could live with being poor';[5] going back to these words can help me to snap back to remembering that I have what I need – it was good enough today, it can still be enough for tomorrow, and I can avoid the marketing trap.

I personally recommend giving yourself a twenty-four-hour pause. This can be a brilliant little hack to help you work out if you're impulsively reacting to an ad, or buying to serve a genuine need. This is especially helpful when shopping online. Put things into your virtual basket, and step away. Sleep on it. Give yourself time to imagine the item in your home, in your life, in your wardrobe. Consider the real-life changes that will occur as a consequence of you going ahead with the purchase. Remember that it's highly likely that there will be systems in place from the business that will email you to remind you that you have an open basket and offering to complete the sale for you. You may even be sent a discount code, but be strong! Do the full amount of time that you have promised to yourself, be it twenty-four hours or three days, whatever it may be to interrupt an impulse buy. If you get to the end of the time period and you still really want it, you're much

THE 'DO-I-NEED-IT?' FILTER

closer to knowing that this was a considered purchase and it's far more likely that you will have set yourself up for a longer lasting relationship with the new thing that you will allow into your life (you may have also managed to gain a discount through the mere act of waiting!) but often, you simply forget that you wanted it. Things move so fast and there will be a different distraction on the horizon.

Shopping for vintage and preloved with a delay can be harder to do because there is a high chance that the thing that you are admiring will be gone if you wait any length of time. In these cases, you can occasionally ask if it can be put aside for a day, or if there is a return policy for you to bring it back without having used it if you need time to decide if it was the right thing for you.

Next, **Affirm** – after you've resisted the initial urge to purchase, what you then need to do is to think again, when you're in a calmer and less impulsive state, about what benefits the new thing is going to bring to your life. Affirm the reasons. Think about the 'job' that the purchase is going to do and why you are considering it still. Physically writing this down is a good step – it will slow you down and force you to be clear about what you think you will be getting from this purchase. External affirmation is a very useful tool too, as long as you ask a person who knows you really well and has an insight into what you have chosen and loved in the past – that is, the things that are quintessentially 'you'. Showing that trusted person and gaining affirmation from them, or honest critique, can be a helpful step in pausing your impulses and helping you to decide if it's the right thing to go for.

Check for **Identical** – go through the other things that

you have that are just like this! Do you already own something that does the same job? Does it need to be revitalised and used again? Can you avoid buying new and resurrect your existing item? There are many times when we are drawn to something that we like because it looks or feels familiar in some way. It's not unusual to realise that this is because you already have something like it that has slipped to the back of your wardrobe or cupboard. Having an edit is such an eye-opener, when you deliberately pull all your clothing / kitchen gadgets / sewing stash / sports kit out of storage and count up what's there; it's surprising to see the things that you had forgotten you had, and it helps you to avoid buying them again without realising that you were duplicating.

And now consider **Themes** – if you are still sure that you want to buy this thing, ask yourself to dive into the daydream you will be having about owning this product. What do you notice about the life you're imagining when it's yours? What else is in the scene? Have you changed other parts of your reality when you have created the daydream? You may be hoping that this purchase is going to 'buy' you more than it's able to offer. Look for the wider themes in your visualisation and be honest with yourself about whether this purchase is going to be able to fulfil them.

After you've been through the WAIT steps, it's time to:

Visualise – now you need to step out of your daydream, back into your present world and visualise the new thing in that world. Place it in your room, or in your hand, or wherever it would be. Imagine having it. Place it into your world and try to observe how things are different when it's

THE 'DO-I-NEED-IT?' FILTER

there. Just be an observer. You're not using the thing, it's just now in your home.

How different is your life? Who is benefitting from it? Who has noticed it? You may find at this point that you start to realise it will make almost no difference at all to own it and, in fact, not having it cluttering up your space and keeping things light feels better.

When the urge to buy strikes, take yourself through the **WAIT, Visualise** steps:

W. Wait at least twenty-four hours. Put it in your basket or leave it in the shop. Walk away for a bit.
A. Affirm your reasons for wanting it. Gain affirmation from a trusted other.
I. Identical – do you already have something that's the same? Why is this different?
T. Themes – what's in your visualisation? What are you really wanting?

Visualise the present reality.

Task: Identifying Your Trigger Moments

I want you to see if you can identify the times when you are most likely to make a purchase that's not going to serve you well; an unnecessary item that will not enrich your life in any discernible way. When are you most likely to fall into unconscious consumerist habits?

_____
_____
_____
_____
_____
_____
_____
_____
_____
_____
_____
_____
_____
_____
_____
_____

THE 'DO-I-NEED-IT?' FILTER

For some people it's a payday reaction; the money has come in so it's natural to immediately buy something. Maybe it's evening absent-minded scrolling that leads you to tap through to an effortless Apple Pay purchase. A glass of wine perhaps loosening the purse-strings? Maybe it's when you spend time with family or friends who appear to have more than you, making you feel that you need to work a bit harder at maintaining the standard. Maybe you have a long commute surrounded by ads and the suggestions are just too hard to ignore, day after day. For some people there are times of the month as well as annual anniversaries that will act as trigger moments for comfort shopping. Being able to spot these patterns in your consumer behaviour is brilliant; the first step in changing something that you're not entirely happy with is working out when and why you're doing it. If you can work out when you're most likely to spend without need or particular joy, you can start to eliminate the likelihood of suffering the consequences of buyer's regret.

It starts to feel empowering to step away. There is a dopamine rush associated with making purchases and yet another when the parcel arrives if bought online, but these feelings can be replaced with the feeling of pride in the self-control of not having to buy things so often. There is undoubtedly a pang of guilt involved in overconsumption and being able to lessen that feeling for ourselves and know that we are finding other ways to be content is a great boost to how we view ourselves, and ultimately to how good we feel.

CHAPTER 5

What to Get Rid of and How

Prepare yourself because this could be a tricky chapter! You've got me with you though, and we're tackling this together.

What to get rid of and how? This is such a difficult question because it's so personal and it's also ever changing; the recycling landscape is adapting and evolving as new ways to process waste materials are either developed and brought into action or, conversely, removed due to policy change and short-term costs.

In general, over the past couple of decades we have become much better at recycling. The Household Waste Recycling Act of 2003 means that local authorities in England have to provide every home with a separate collection of at least two types of recyclable materials by 2010 and over that time we've learnt to stop throwing everything into black bin bags. I remember a time, at uni in the nineties, when we would think it normal to throw bottles, cans, jars, card, food waste, anything straight into the bin and shove it outside without a second thought. We no longer leave it up to a solitary few to wash containers, peel labels off, strip them into separate components and put them out for recycling. In fact, according to the excellent website www.recyclenow.com, a recent recycling tracker showed that nine in ten UK residents recycle either most, or everything they can.[1] Managing the smaller, daily flow of materials is something that we have adapted well to, and our systems have developed ways of supporting this that will hopefully continue to improve. What we are less good at is dealing with the bigger items – the clothes, furniture, shoes, and myriad household objects that we bring in and later realise we don't want for ever.

In the five years that followed that awful day when our lives were turned upside down, I moved house six times. Every single thing was packed up and shoved around, it was stored and carried, unboxed, re-boxed and stashed away, time and time again. I had to find a way to get the life-stuff of a four-bedroomed house into the tiny flat where I now live. Each move was a stage in a series of editing down my belongings, which meant I had to work out what to get rid of, and how.

With the smaller stuff, we've long been reliant on offloading our clutter in a 'guilt-free' way via the many charity shops that populate our towns and cities, but with their greater visibility has come our greater awareness of the role that these shops are playing in acting as our perceived panacea for all of this clutter. The charity shops renting spaces on our high streets, paying rates and wages and bills are not only given clean and decent contributions – we all bear witness to the fact that frequently, bin bags stuffed with junk are just dumped outside during closed hours, often getting soaked with rain, or far worse, falling foul to late-night pub crawlers and the general lack of public conveniences. Charity shops have to use landfill too; they don't have access to a magical recycling fairy who can take every last bit of broken, dirty tat and break it into wholesome chunks of resource ready to gift back to a community. They have to rent a massive bin and pay for the waste management services of a private company.

It's easy to allow yourself to believe that all charity shops will be grateful for your contributions, but when they are used by people to dispose of unwanted items that the donors know are clearly not going to sell – broken things, items with pieces missing, stained materials – then what is happening is simply a transference of a problem. A donor can walk off feeling virtuous after taking their stuff to a charity shop, but if they know that deep down, in that bag of donations, they have buried some problems, then they are only fooling themselves. It would be more virtuous to have put it straight into landfill rather than offsetting the guilt, the responsibility and the cost to someone else.

Obviously there are good ways to dispose of things, or at least 'better' ways when the right resources are available, but what it really boils down to is the fact that we need to be far more mindful from the beginning about what we're allowing into our homes; the constant in and out, the flushing through of all these things that we are buying, is not at all sustainable in terms of long-term global waste management, even if our personal budgets can cope. Waste is expensive. We need to remember that there is no such place as 'away' for us to throw things to; someone or somewhere is paying the price. Whether to landfill, where there are 540 sites still operational in the UK, or to incinerators, where nearly half of all UK waste is burnt, the stuff we get rid of has a massive impact on our environment and it takes a multi-billion-pound industry to manage it all. We humans are always going to produce rubbish, there is no way around this; archaeology has long found the clue-rich midden heaps not too far from the greatest treasures of communities past, but what has happened during our watch is that the rate of consumption has accelerated to a point where the discard is overwhelming. We have no choice but to slow it down.

The encouraging realisation is that despite it feeling discomfiting to think about all that we used and slung away in the past, we have a great opportunity now to put the brakes on in a really positive way and to continue living our pleasurable lives without the previous level of excess and its difficult consequences. We can build new longer-lasting relationships with our possessions and we can become far more discerning about what will make the grade and be invited into our home in the future.

Firstly, let's consider the different ways in which we decide what things we no longer want, and then we can consider a few options for trying to move them on in the most helpful, least harmful way possible. We can use the age-old wisdom of William Morris, 'Have nothing in your houses that you do not know to be useful, or believe to be beautiful,'[2] which, upon hearing for the first time, I thought it was pretty extreme, but what a wonderful starting point for helping us to see what matters. If you are hanging onto something that falls outside of those categories, unless it's packing some true sentimental heavyweight for you, you probably should be asking yourself why, indeed, you have it at all?

Things that you have taken possession of, that you are going to give space to in your home, should either be useful (and on that, be careful of objects which only have one use – more on that later), or be beautiful, in that they bring something to you by their very nature of being. They bring you joy – the aesthetic enrichment of having them add decoration to your life has a positive effect on you. I would also add to this, things which hold a high level of emotional attachment; these can be things you don't use daily, or even find attractive, but they are important to you because they link you to a special time, place or person.

Which of your possessions would you place into each section? And which would fall outside of any?

Task: Worth Keeping

Which of your possessions would you place into each section? And which would fall outside of any?

Sometimes we do hang onto things that fulfil none of these roles in our lives and it is this excess of stuff that we term as 'clutter'. It can feel as though we're in a permanent state of trying to de-clutter our homes, that we allow in many more things than we need, and certainly many more things than we believe to be useful or beautiful. We need to start thinking about how we've got into the habit of unconscious accumulation, and how we can try to stop it happening.

WHAT TO GET RID OF AND HOW

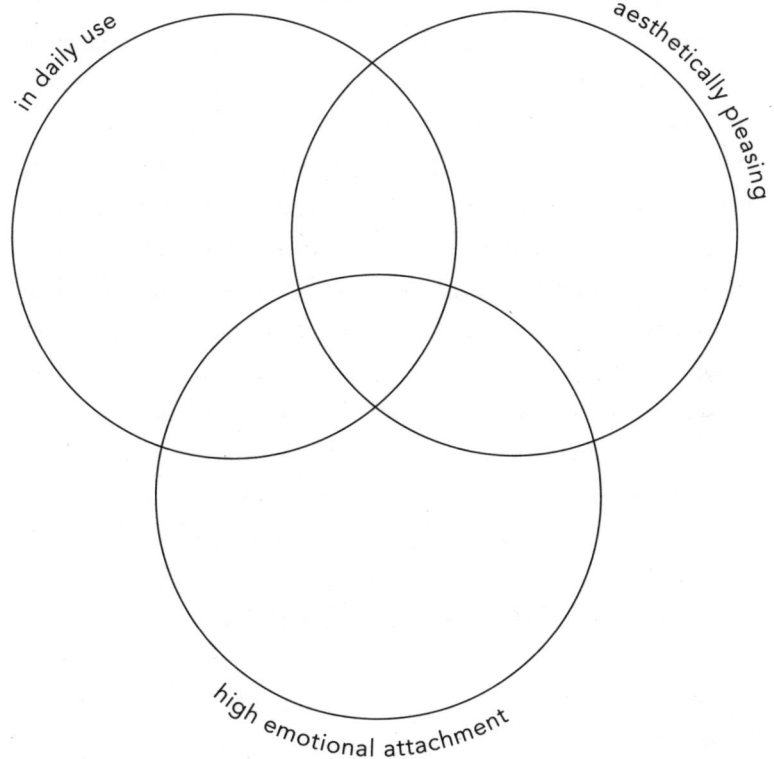

An easy starting point would be to identify any items that only have one specific and fixed application, which you rarely use. I first started thinking about this when I was in a well-known budget supermarket a while back and the middle aisle had a cooking-themed week with lots of different electrical kitchen gadgets at low cost, enticing the ordinary weekly shoppers who had entered only with the intention of getting food, into picking up what seemed a fabulous bargain to make fancy culinary things at home. One of the appliances on offer was a waffle maker that had

Teflon plates inside, which would shape your batter into a professional-looking waffle. I thought this was wonderful and I picked it up, daydreaming about a weekend morning when I could whip up these convincing-looking waffles and top them with fresh raspberries to win 'mum of the week' (I'm only competing with myself here and the many versions of mum that I can be). However, my partner, who was shopping alongside me, pointed out that in essence, the wonderful fancy waffle maker did exactly the same job as the sandwich toaster that I already had in my cupboard. It was a small electrical counter-top heater with removable plates that form, or mould, a set shape while heating what's inside. I could make triangular waffles in the sandwich toaster, they would taste just as good, providing I got the quantity right. So I already had all the tools I needed to create a waffle if that's what I wanted to do.

I guess at that point I realised that you can fill your kitchen, your house, your life, with a host of single-use gadgets with highly specific agendas that you will rarely ever employ, or, you can try to find those precious base items that are applicable to many tasks and build a core set of wonderful tools that you look after and get millions of uses from. The same can be said of cosmetics, cleaning products, and of course, our clothes. Most of the time we will have no need for highly specific concoctions of any sort when basic multi-use options will do the job. Plus, there's a growing realisation that we can actually make a lot of our own products from simple, cheap and non-toxic ingredients (I highly recommend giving @nancybirtwhistle a follow for her superb green, clean recipes for all of your household needs).

WHAT TO GET RID OF AND HOW

Task: Monofunctional Miscellany

Let's take a minute to have a think about what we might be storing unnecessarily. Can you identify any gadgets in your home which serve only one specific task that can be done by something else and that you're not using regularly?

The sorts of things that will be in this box are the things that we buy on a whim, use for three days and then leave to collect dust at the back of a cupboard: rice maker / popcorn maker / microwave egg poacher / electric egg boiler / hot dog maker / salad spinner / cupcake maker / make-up brush cleanser . . .

It's good to let these things go, but even better to become aware of why you don't need them so that you don't make the same buying mistake again.

Write out anything you can think of in the box below.

WHAT TO GET RID OF

When I think about de-cluttering, my mind immediately goes to the kitchen, but there are places all over the house that will need to be assessed. Let's go through a few key areas of the home and consider what can go:

Garages and Loft Spaces

A lot of us use the garage or loft as a limbo zone for our stuff. Stuff that we know that we don't need close by anymore; we've had our time with it and now it needs to be out of our daily environment, but we delay making any real hard decisions by shoving it off into those spaces. Bag it up, slide the door down and forget about it for a year or two. Sometimes it feels like the only way to manage those big 'clear-out' days when the mood occasionally strikes (the times when you unintentionally go from matching a few odd socks up to pulling out every last item from under your bed, behind your drawers and from the bottom of the airing cupboard) is to dump stuff into the limbo spaces and offset the decisions.

If you have more than one child, it's highly likely that you will want to hang onto most of the outgrown stuff from number one, and you'll bag it up with every intention of remembering where it all is. If you are dealing with stuff that took you a long time to save up for, such as sports equipment for an activity you rarely do anymore, a former collection of something, seasonal stuff, there's a really high chance that you will not want to get rid of it. Having these storage spaces in our lives allows us to play a trump card – the 'Not Going to Deal With it' card. It takes a long time and a lot of energy to unfetter yourself from a lifetime of stuff, especially if you are going to do it in a considered way. I don't know anyone with access to a garage, shed or loft who hasn't filled it with the articles of life they don't want, but don't want to face the not wanting of.

The bottom line is, we have to get in there and be brave. The stuff in boxes for 'later', where the chance of later ever materialising is pretty slim. If you've held onto something for over a year, through all the seasons and you have not needed it once, there's a good chance that you could let it go now. Anything that you are genuinely surprised to see when you open up the box again, that can go – you were living a perfectly happy life without even realising it was there. A great tip I heard about for all the beautiful (and not so beautiful) artwork your kids might have made when they were little, is to take photos of them and store in a folder on your phone. Perfect for a long train journey when you're feeling nostalgic and want a good laugh!

Just like the basements of the British Museum, the Metropolitan, or the Louvre, we too have collected more of life's artefacts than we have the space in our homes for, so we have garages, eves, attics and outbuildings where we stash things away and forget about them. The irony is, we keep on collecting. With what's generally considered to be luck, we move up the housing ladder a few times in our adult lives, inhabiting bigger and bigger spaces with more potential to put more things into, and we keep adding. People even rent storage to house some of the stuff they can't fit inside their own four walls, and yet they keep adding. They head off at weekends to spend money in IKEA buying storage solutions in order to be able to store all the things that take up the space that they've spent money on.

There's a lesson to be taken from a well-loved childhood tale here – remember Goldilocks? Although pretty rogue in her criminal breaking and entering of the bears' home, she taught us that there's usually one thing that we love above all the others: one spoon, one bowl, one seat, one mug and when we identify it, when we find our 'perfect one', it seems a whole lot easier to allow the others to slide away and live other lives where they may be perfect for someone else.

We really don't need half as much as we think we do. And if we're able to start to let go without re-filling, we often gain a real sense of freedom and calm.

Kitchen

Food waste is a massive deal and although it's not the same as clutter, it's a real issue for the majority of households. In the UK, we throw away 9.5 million tonnes of food a year and if that's too baffling to comprehend as an amount, just know that globally, we waste a third of all food that's produced.[3] That's across all sectors – production, manufacturing, hospitality, trade, and household – but the latter, us in our homes, makes up 70 per cent of that figure. It's a massive problem for waste management; the environmental consequences are adding millions of tonnes of greenhouse gases to the atmosphere, and distressingly, the edible food that gets binned is enough to have fed every single one of the 8.5 million people in the UK living in food poverty. The average household in the UK will spend just shy of £500 a year on this wasted food that no one will eat, food that will be thrown out, and of that discarded food, it's estimated that over 60 per cent of it was still perfectly edible.[4]

When you're looking through the kitchen, before you give anything away, make sure that you hang onto a decent container for your food compost. Try a couple of weeks of menu planning to see if that helps you to reduce kitchen waste and, if you live in a place where there are affordable shops close enough, trying to do a 'big basics shop' less frequently, but instead, buy the key meal components closer to the time that you will use them are both tried and tested ways of seriously reducing the amount of food that will end up being wasted.

Having lived in a very small flat for the greater part of the last decade, and one where the whole living space is one room acting as entrance, hallway, kitchen, lounge and diner, I have had to find a way to have all things that you might want or need, all in one space, where all is visible from wherever you are. You see the fridge from the sofa. You see the coats from the microwave. You see the front door from the dining table. (Actually, there is no dining table, there's half a dining table. My old dining table was sawn in half and used as a 'breakfast bar' as there was no room for a table in the flat.) In this tight space it became important not to fill up the few cupboards with unnecessary clutter. There is no space for specific pans, so the few I have are all-rounders. There are enough plates and cups for all of us, but not enough to host a party. There are no wine glasses. There are no gadgets that only do one job (unless you count toasters? I don't, but you probably could). There are no fancy boiling water taps, wine fridges, ice-cream makers or citrus juicers; there's pretty much just the basic kit that you might take camping, and it seems to be enough to make all the things that we need to make.

As you would expect, there is a total mismatch of crockery. This has never caused an issue; the King has never decided to drop by, and his mother didn't either. I would really recommend letting go of the idea of having a matching set of stuff. If one thing gets broken, it's never an issue to replace it and you will never get to a point where you feel that your set is outdated and needs replacing. It simply exists, evolves and different people can have their own favourite things.

Bathroom

To start with, I would urge you to cut right back on the number of personal care products that you buy. Most of the time we don't need much more than a detergent item for cleansing (I could go on for way too long about my love of bars of soap), perhaps a conditioner, perhaps shaving cream, and some kind of toothpaste and deodorant. Of course, there are thousands of other lotions and potions that we like, and we have become used to, but try to go through your bathroom cupboards, shelves and baskets and have a major edit. See what you can live without for a couple of weeks and then make it a habit to not buy more.

Challenge yourself to use all of everything, cut those

tubes in half, scrape those jars, squeeze the containers. Use less. Scale it all down if you are able. Pick as many reusable consumables as you can: face cloths, cleaning cloths, fabric make-up removal pads, sanitary products. All these switches from the disposable versions become very ordinary over time and will save not only the waste from being created, but the money you will spend over and over again in buying them every week.

Clothing

This is a massive area of opportunity for most of us. Our clothes are our outward expression of ourselves and are hugely important in telling our story as we move through our lives. We define ourselves by what we wear; we show other people our styles and we are also showing them our allegiances and our values. So many messages are conveyed by what we wear and how we wear it. No wonder then, that it has become something that we, as a society, are addicted to spending money on. However, we have reached a stage where we have so much more than we need, and we are treating something that used to be precious and cared for with an attitude of disposability. We have created a global system where we don't have to face the real consequences of fast fashion because we ship our ruined and wasted textiles away, back to the global south to become the waste problem of others. We must be brave and face up to our overconsumption.

Building a much better relationship with clothes is essential, and we will discuss this in more detail in Chapter 6, but for now, it's a great idea to clear your decks in readiness and to remove the clothes that you have built no relationship with; if they are not being worn, if they do not fit, if they hold no memory, they will not be missed – let them go! The coat-hanger trick is an old favourite here – for things hanging in your wardrobe, you just make sure that each time you wear something and hang it back up, you turn the hook of the hanger to face the other way to the rest of the clothes. This way, at the end of a certain time period, you're able to easily identify all the things that you have worn, and more crucially, all the things that you are not ever picking out.

When you're having your clear-out, make sure to include anything that you bought just to please someone else, and anything that you bought for your pretend life – you know the one I'm talking about! I used to trip up and buy for the pretend me too often; I have subsequently realised she doesn't exist, but the real me is worth investing in. I have changed, managing to stop myself from picking up way too many 'event dresses' for all the events I never go to, and instead focusing on items that will actually enhance my daily life, like my beloved short wellies and a big, warm fleece.

Books, CDs and DVDs

If you have ever listened to BBC Radio 4's 'Desert Island Discs', where the guest has to choose eight tracks, a book and one luxury item to have on an imaginary desert island for evermore, you will know how impossible it feels to most guests to whittle down the emotive musical soundtrack of their lives into just eight records to keep for life. It's a process that they go through as they talk to the presenter, remembering the soundscape of their childhood, the fabric of their teenage fight for freedom and the songs that have got them through the best and worst times of their lives. These are the songs that we should keep. It's far too personal for anyone else to suggest what's worth keeping and what is not, but when it comes to music, all I will say is there is something solid and grounding for us as humans to be able to touch and hold our music via a record, or the box of a cassette or CD. Our cars still use them (as I write this, my car still has a cassette player) so it's worth still hanging onto those physical music items that are meaningful for you. It's difficult to explain, but I believe that there's a different quality to non-digitally streamed music and there is definitely a certain discipline, or focus, that's required to give yourself to that one whole album without deviating to something else that pops up and tries to grab your attention.

Similarly, films tend to either grab us fully, or not mean much at all, and we only need to keep hard copies of those that you feel you would miss were you never able to stream them. Creating a little zip-up wallet of your personal blockbusters on DVD would be a fun way to clear out the flops and enable you to curate your 'forever film' selection.

I have a similar feeling about books; you will know which ones are a part of you, and you may be one of the many people who feel that books form an essential part of the backdrop of your home. There will be a few books that feel crucial to you, your 'core collection', ones you would feel a little bereft without, but it can also be true that you are holding onto dozens of titles that you have no particular emotional attachment to and that you will never read again. You may be giving precious shelf or storage space to a heavy load of books that mean very little to you; you'll simply end up moving them from one home to another without a reason. You can feel guilt-free about giving these away; remember that books can have a wonderful life of their own travelling from one reader to another – sharing stories is a beautiful thing and some of the titles that are not your core collection might go on to become more precious to another person. For added joy, when giving away books, you can write a little message for the new reader about what you loved (no plot spoilers!) onto a paper bookmark and slip it in-between the pages for them to find.

Old Toys

For households where children are growing up, or have grown up, the signs of those precious days manifest in the usual ways: the ubiquitous red and yellow plastic car in the garden now with one damaged wheel, the mildewing basketball hoop bolted to the wall, the cupboard with a pile of incomplete games with one split side to the box and the drawer full of dried felt-tip pens. There is an absolute abundance of stuff that comes with child-rearing, some of which will become the most-prized of all your life's treasures, while some of it is just massive tat which you are allowed to breathe a huge sigh of relief upon relinquishing.

Clean up and move the massive tat on. If the children are not using it anymore, let it go.

As with the books and music and clothes, there will be some things that you do not feel prepared to part with, but these will be few (and hopefully, small). Take photos as you release them; often it feels enough to have a picture stored for those future moments when you want to look back and reminisce about the Build-A-Bear gang, the magnetic sand tray phase or the L.O.L. doll obsession. I bought a couple of multi-paged clear plastic document folder-books and used one for each child to store their little drawings and certificates in – too many to frame but certainly not anything that I was willing to throw into the recycling.

No one is guaranteed a future of their own design, but I have to admit that a very few precious things from my days as a mum of young children have been kept in case I have the luck to become a grandparent, or an older person who gets to welcome children to my home. These are the truly delightful things that I know will stand the test of time, things I fell in love with when my children were tiny, and I wasn't able to pass on: the heirloom items. They don't take up much space: a few adorable Sylvanians, some beautiful picture books and a good weight of, by now, very old Lego.

These are just some of the key areas of the home and of the thousands of the 'articles of stufferation' that we draw into our lives without regularly editing. Setting yourself the challenge of letting go of the things that you do identify as superfluous, will bring you a real sense of satisfaction and will help you to see that living with less is genuinely good for your well-being.

Right, we have a good idea of what things we can start to let go of, but what are our alternatives for moving things along without resorting to landfill? Time to consider the options for a clear out:

Giving to Family and Friends

This should be your first port of call. It's what's known as 'mindful rehoming'. Asking the friend who previously showed an interest in something, or the family member who has a need for something you're passing along, is a great way of making sure that your stuff finds an appropriate new home. Friends are much more likely to take and use something that they know the provenance of, rather than looking to find it from a stranger. It feels a lot 'safer' for most people starting out as second-hand users to have things that originated in homes that they know. It can also create an important sense of community and connection for you and it minimises extra transportation cost factors when you can drop things off locally, or as you drop over to see people.

Upcycling

Is there another use for it? Can you look at it in a different way? Sir Ken Robinson, one of the most wonderful leaders on creativity and education, championed a simple experiment into divergent thinking where people across different age groups were given a paperclip and were asked to list all the things it was, or could be used for. The average well-educated adult could find between ten and fifteen things that the paperclip could 'be', while the children of kindergarten age were able to come up with 200 plus. Sir Ken argued that in the most part, we have a latent creativity which is educated out of us as we are taught what is correct and true.[5] The kids in the paperclip test were operating at 'genius level' because they had yet to learn that a paperclip is a paperclip and only a paperclip. People who are brilliant at upcycling are like the kindergarten cohort – they are able to look at things in a flexible way and consider what other uses there could be for those materials. Could the wooden crate become a bedside table? Could the cotton duvet cover be made into a blouse? Could the basket be turned into a lamp? If there is something you own, that you like the aesthetic of, but serves no purpose in your home in its current form, just try reframing its job to see if there is another role it could take up with a few tweaks. This is where Pinterest comes in as an invaluable tool; typing 'upcycled anything' into a Pinterest search will give you a really good visual guide as to what you could aim for.

Facebook Groups

Local Facebook community groups are brilliant places to find and to pass on larger bulky things that may be too difficult to post and are not wanted by anyone you've asked. Each local group will have their own rules for buying and selling that you will usually find on the noticeboard but there are a couple of general tips that will help you to use this type of Facebook group service well, both as a seller and as a buyer. Turning your notifications on for the group is helpful so that you are the first to know about the items on offer. You can select to be notified about every post in the group (probably a bit extreme) or you can set it to let you know only when friends or family have posted something, or a mixture of both to allow highlights of the group.

When decent stuff is advertised (a fabulous barely used sofa bed, for example), you need to be really fast to get into the queue of people who comment, and therefore are staking their place in the line, but do not lose heart if you're not the first. People comment to secure their place in the queue and often later discover that they have no way of collecting the thing, or that their room is too small, and the offer will work its way down the list and maybe get to you. When you're using the group to post your own item, experience teaches that when you offer something for free, you are much more likely to have comments from people who say they want it, and then don't turn up. If you place a modest value on something, something of a filter happens naturally; you have declared it to have a value and people respond by treating it as something with value and they will make a commitment to collect.

Always set your boundaries with collections from the outset; it's very annoying to be trying to de-clutter by advertising decent stuff for a tiny price, and then finding that, as you were not clear about collection times, the person who said they wanted it isn't able to get to you until a week next Thursday when they borrow a van from their uncle's mate, and they're now asking you if you can hang on until then. Always be clear in the initial post and state that you have a date and time by which it must be collected, or you will move to the next person in the list.

Vinted and eBay

Online selling platforms are fabulous for things that can be easily named, are from a recognised brand or with specific identities that can be searched for. You don't do so well if it's a random wooden shelf, or a plain cotton top as those as keywords would make the search so broad that your item will be entirely lost in the billion listings that fill the preloved space at any one time. If you are able to give the brand, and perhaps the specific item name, even if it's just one or two parts of a set, then the chances are that someone, somewhere, will be entering those exact terms into their search and they will strike gold when they see your listing. Make sure that you read the fulfilment and shipping options really carefully; it can catch you out to realise that you will have, by default, committed to shipping within a certain date and you may have offered a range of options that your buyer is able to choose from, including click and collect drop-off services as well as standard postal. There will be settings as you set up your seller account that you need to read through to be sure that you're comfortable with the options that you'll be offering when your sales transactions go through.

Looking at eBay and apps like Vinted can be very useful in gaining an idea about the accepted monetary value of the things you are looking to sell – to help you know what would be the right amount to ask for.

Home Sales and Car Boots

Garage sales, yard sales and car boot sales are a great way to move on a load of stuff in one hit. These types of sales attract buyers looking for a real bargain, so it's the perfect place to get rid of things that you are happy to part with for a few pounds and it's definitely not where you would want to start negotiations for the antique family silver. Spreading your stuff out over your driveway or doorstep, or setting it all up in a field on some crazily early morning is a high-intensity way of cleaning out and will demand a lot of energy in one blast. It's good to bear in mind that you may have to let things go for less than you think they're worth and see it more as recycling than profit-based, and you may be left with a load of unsold stuff that you still have to deal with. On the good side, however, if you price it right and perhaps even give things away at the end, you will find that it's a wonderful way to move on those odd and bulky things that prove too low value to list and post to strangers, and too good to be destined for the rubbish. It can also be a fabulously fun day of meeting people and building connections in your community. Remember to have a decent float of change available if you're selling, or have your PayPal account ready to accept digital payments and the buyer can ping it through on the spot.

Charity Shops
I have deliberately placed this go-to option quite far down the list, not because I want to undermine their role in communities, but because we need to stop using them to get rid of the cruddy things that we would not pass on in other ways. Yes, do use them for really good items that you know will hold some worth and value, but please do consider whether you are relying on that swoop and drop to dump bags of things that you know are not really worth steaming for the rails.

Also, it's often worth phoning ahead on the day to check if the shop you're planning to donate to is taking things in. Charity shops frequently have to put a halt onto accepting new things as they struggle to sort and store what's already arrived and it can feel very annoying to get your stuff all cleaned, folded and packed for a drop-off, only to park up and lug it across town and find you have to turn around and put it back in the car boot again (where it will stay for the next two months). Remember too, that it's quite rare for a charity shop to be able to accept electrical items, and it's worth calling a few of the larger shops in your area to determine whether or not they have a branch which can accept larger items of furniture if you would like to try to rehome bigger things.

Schools, Nurseries and Shelters
Finally, a reminder that there are institutions around in need of certain resources and it's good to check in with them if you think that your offering might be useful. This is different from

a charity shop taking in stuff to sell; this is direct donations to support the actions of the group. For example, schools and nurseries can often use craft materials for art sessions, or gardening surplus for their grounds. Animal shelters make good use of older bedding and towels that would no longer be chosen by people in charity shops, and shelters for people frequently need decent unused toiletries and good, smart workwear for supporting clients getting back into the routine of interviews and employment.

Lastly, before we throw anything out, it should be our goal to make sure that we're not getting rid of it due to an easily mendable fault or break. Just as we have become better at consuming, we've become increasingly de-skilled and less likely to try to mend things. This is not entirely our fault; it's widely regarded as the truth that objects are being designed with planned obsolescence as well as with a lack of easily replaceable parts. The more times that we are forced to buy a new version, the longer a company's shareholders can maximise the profits they get from us – why have a customer only buying once, when they could be kept on board as a repeat purchaser?

We are now in an age where schools no longer have the curriculum time for 'household' skills, such as home economics for meal preparation and basic nutrition, metal work, woodwork and needlework – all skills that used to have some degree of instruction in the classroom. There is a massive amount of skill held within the hands of the older generation; you only need to visit one of the wonderful local Repair Cafés of the growing international movement, to see the menders at work and to realise what resourceful talent lies with your community elders – try to learn from their experience if you can. Here's a small list of household tools that will help you to have a basic kit at hand so that you can try to 'Fix First' – use YouTube videos to guide you; they are plentiful and freely available when you can access the internet.

- A few needles / A few basic colours of thread / Pins / Scissors / Spare buttons / Wonderweb. These basics will allow you to stitch up, or iron up, a dropped hem, fix a lost button or mend a split seam with a few careful stitches.

- Wood glue / Superglue / Glue gun / A few steel spring clamps. The basics for glueing broken things where you have both / all parts still to hand.

- Screwdrivers. A few assorted sizes, both slotted and Phillips. So many simple repair and maintenance jobs will require covers to be removed with screwdrivers, etc.

- Allen / Hex key set. Many tightening/loosening jobs can be done with these, and you'll definitely need them if you ever have to make or dismantle IKEA furniture.

NOT NEEDING NEW

- Hammer. Thousands of uses, although I mostly use mine for hanging pictures and opening coconuts.

- Adjustable spanner. This will enable you to undertake simple plumbing tasks, like removing a tap to change a washer, or tightening nuts used to hold a table or chairs together, etc.

- Battery charger / USB plugs. A few rechargeable batteries and a simple charger will mean you can keep using little devices like fairy lights and small radios, etc., even when so many things are switched to micro-USB.

- Can of WD-40. This legendary stuff has over 2,000 uses according to the manufacturers. The product name literally stands for 'Water Displacing, 40th formula'; it can protect metals, de-grease, loosen, stop creaks and squeaks by lubricating joints, prevent rust, drive water from tools, shine stainless steel – loads of opportunities to use it when fixing things and a great addition to your household toolkit.

- Duct tape. A woven cotton-backed tape first used for military purposes in the Second World War, now applied to millions of situations where you need to have a quick, waterproof adhesive tape fix. Definitely one to keep at hand around your home as a temporary mend for many occasions.

- Plunger. A simple suction cup with a handle, great for unblocking drains in your basins, sinks, baths and shower trays via a bit of pressure and force to pump air in and out, and release any build-ups of fat, soap or hair which are prone to accumulate in U-bends and cause plumbing problems.

- Crow bar. A fantastic tool, which has picked up a bit of an unfairly bad reputation from bank-robber stories, but when I was involved in the gutting and refurbishment of my flat, the crow bar and I became great workmates. Used to prise things away, lift things, chisel away at old flooring, remove carpet gripper rods, skirting boards, etc.

Building up a basic set of your own tools that you feel confident with will really help you to see mending as your primary port of call and will support you in being able to consume less, waste less and save money. Win–win!

Task: Commit to a De-clutter

If this chapter has made you realise you can get rid of something, now is the time to make a plan. I urge you to get your diary out, paper or digital, and commit yourself to a de-clutter. Decide where you will start, be realistic and specific. Make it manageable. Perhaps take one drawer at a time, one side of a cupboard, one shelf in the garage, one bag in the loft.

If you bite off small chunks and you can start to see that it *is* possible, that you *are* able to cope and that you will feel a real sense of achievement in having sorted out that one nagging area of clutter, it will become something that you will be able to face with greater ease and you will have the freedom from stuff that you desire. So, have a think, write it in the diary . . .

WHAT are you clearing out? WHERE is it? WHEN will you do it? Plan it now!

WHAT TO GET RID OF AND HOW

Part Two

CHAPTER 6

Fashion v. Style

Right! Now that we have been through Part One of *Not Needing New* and ascertained that there are loads of things that we can do to edit out the unnecessary, and to curb the craving to add more and more, let's dive into Part Two. We're kicking off with the subject that triggered my whole exploration into the wonderful world of preloved: clothes!

In the modern day, clothes and fashion have become a way to show our sustainable values and our ability to avoid buying *new*. There is so much judgement about what we wear and it's hard to avoid that critique since your clothes are the primary way you or I can present ourselves in the world. No matter what you choose, some sort of message will be gleaned by anyone who is meeting you, whether you consciously intended to send a message or not.

There are obvious sartorial subcultures: Goth, Preppy, Bohemian, Punk, Cottagecore, Minimalist, etc., but even if you don't subscribe to any defined group, you will be constantly sending out subtle, ever-changing messages by your daily clothing choices; it could be 'business', 'gym fan', 'allotment owner', 'school run'. It's surprising how these little clues send out big messages and it's really interesting to spot these and to play with them. What I have learnt over time is that we can define ourselves in whatever ways we wish without having to continually buy into the latest ubiquitous 'drops' offered by the high street and via online fast-fashion retailers.

The key points for us to delve into in this chapter deal not so much with where to buy good preloved clothes, but rather why opting for fewer and better, and specifically for preloved, will have absolutely no negative effects on your perceived level of style. Two major pillars here: 1. Style is not the same as fashion, and 2. Second-hand is NOT second-best.

Before we dive in, let's first try to understand some of the difficulties that people may experience in feeling wholly comfortable with second-hand, or with 'other people's clothes'.

Firstly, for anyone who grew up in clothes-poverty, it makes perfect sense why you may want to break away from the memory of that experience and nurture yourself, and those you love, with the gift of your own, new, self-chosen clothes. That choice may feel incredibly healing and lead to a strong sense of acceptance and safety. The shame that comes with having to wear outdated or ill-fitting clothes in school environments when you're young is a lasting one. Children do not hold back with their words and as a teacher I have seen this first-hand. I want to make it very clear that I'm not telling anyone who has coped with the impact of poverty that they need to embrace second-hand if it doesn't feel good. There are lots of wonderful and sustainable ways to choose new things carefully, to treat them well, and hold onto them for years. These could be fantastic routes for anyone recovering from these kinds of childhood challenges. Very fortunately for me, this wasn't my experience, which has meant that I haven't had that obstacle to manage.

If this also wasn't your experience, there may still be a barrier to second-hand due to a fairly widely held belief that second-hand clothes are 'dirty' or 'undesirable'. After some reflection, I believe this is partly an historic stigma that we have accepted as a truth for our times without fully exploring it. It's easy to understand why it feels awkward, uncomfortable or somehow cringy to put something next to your skin that may have been so close to another human you know nothing about. You may start to picture your worst fears around the hygiene standards of the former owner. It's not unusual to feel worried about this and to reject the idea of anything second-hand due to the inability to know exactly who first had it and how it was treated. However, the massive increase in preloved clothes sales in the UK over the past few years (according to GlobalData, the clothes resale market in the UK grew by 149 per cent between 2016 and 2022 and is on track to rise by 67.5 per cent from 2022 to 2026)[1] has seen second-hand sales being dealt with in a whole new way. Gone are the days when a bin liner of mixed, worn-out-wear would come back from the local jumble sale for a matter of pennies. We now see national charities opening shops in well-heeled high streets that are decked out like independent boutiques. The aesthetic is both organised and luxurious, the processes that the clothes go through before they are put out onto the shopfloor eliminates anything unfit for resale and will usually ensure that each piece is completely clean and has been steamed.

It's becoming far more socially normal to engage in reselling and redistributing clothes as we each have so much more than we have ever had (it's roughly estimated that we have five times the amount of clothing per person than we did in the eighties);[2] this increase in volume means that what makes its way to the rails of a charity shop today isn't the musty old final offering before a garment is consigned to a rag bag – it's far more likely to be something barely worn from the wardrobe of someone, just like you, who has realised that for whatever reason, they bought something that they are not getting good use from, and they would rather have the space back.

It's also good to remember that if you do step into the world of preloved and buy any clothes, you can choose to put the clothes through your own favourite washing/cleaning process as reassurance that they begin a new, fresh life with you. You are in charge here; you get to wash it until you're happy that it's good to go for you.

And let's also not forget that with brand-new clothes sales, there's no guarantee that your item has not been tried on and returned to sale. There are many points at which an item of clothing will be handled and will be exposed to chemical, as well as human, contamination as it passes through the manufacturing, packing and transportation mechanisms.

It seems to me to be really important that we overcome this mindset, which is surely contributing to the fact that there are five times as many clothes per capita as there were in the eighties and it's not slowing down. The UN Environment

Programme figures estimate that today people buy 60 per cent more clothes than in any previous generation, and will only wear them for half as long as we used to.[3] Over the past fifteen years, fashion consumption has more than doubled, the quality and longevity of the clothes has seen an undeniable decline, and the number of times a garment is worn before being discarded has decreased by 36 per cent.[4] This huge change has been fed by a massive industry pushing and persuading us to buy this inferior offering more frequently, by the increased use of cheap petrochemical fabrics like polyester and nylon allowing the rise of ultra-fast fashion and micro-trends, and by cheap overseas labour markets enabling decreasing prices. In the early nineties, Americans bought an average of forty garments per person each year. By the mid-2000s this had leapt up to seventy garments per person per year.[5] The story of this 'consume and discard' boom is played out in the engorged waste streams; charity shops and resellers are flooded with stock where much of it is barely worn. The argument that second-hand clothes are scrappy, dirty or worn out, simply by nature of having first belonged to another person, no longer stands. Where, once, it might have been the case that charity shops were offered tired, musty donations of 'dead people's suits', our modern obsession with wearing a new garment for each new, significant outing has created an entirely different waste-scape. What we now tend to see is a far greater volume of barely worn textiles being rammed through the donations channels, with a significantly lower quality of garment.

As our clothes are made more quickly, at higher volumes, with tighter profit margins, using cheaper fabrics, the attention to detail has fallen away. Whereas you may have spotted signs of good tailoring on vintage high street clothing – a high stitch count, flat seams with an allowance for alterations, the little details like a stem of thread for correct button positioning, print patterns that match at the seams – you are unlikely to find the same craftsmanship on current high street offerings. Clothes which have been made well are much more likely to last, and to survive being passed from one person to another; they cope better with the inevitable wear of washing and drying, and the more prevalent past use of good-quality fabrics with higher thread counts makes garments both hang better upon the wearer, and provide greater warmth and comfort.

These are all reasons why genuine vintage garments are prized and why they frequently command good prices when resold. The value that was created when they were made, the value that was stitched into them, remains. You may have an experience of the value that can sit within a piece of clothing. Let's try to get a personal sense of the value within well-made things:

Task: Good Quality Clothing

Think of an item of clothing that you have now, or have had in the past, that you would identify as really well made. Apart from price, how do you know that it's good quality? Use the labels to describe any details about the physical feel, the design, the materials that made it so good and also consider the emotional value that you gain from owning and wearing it.

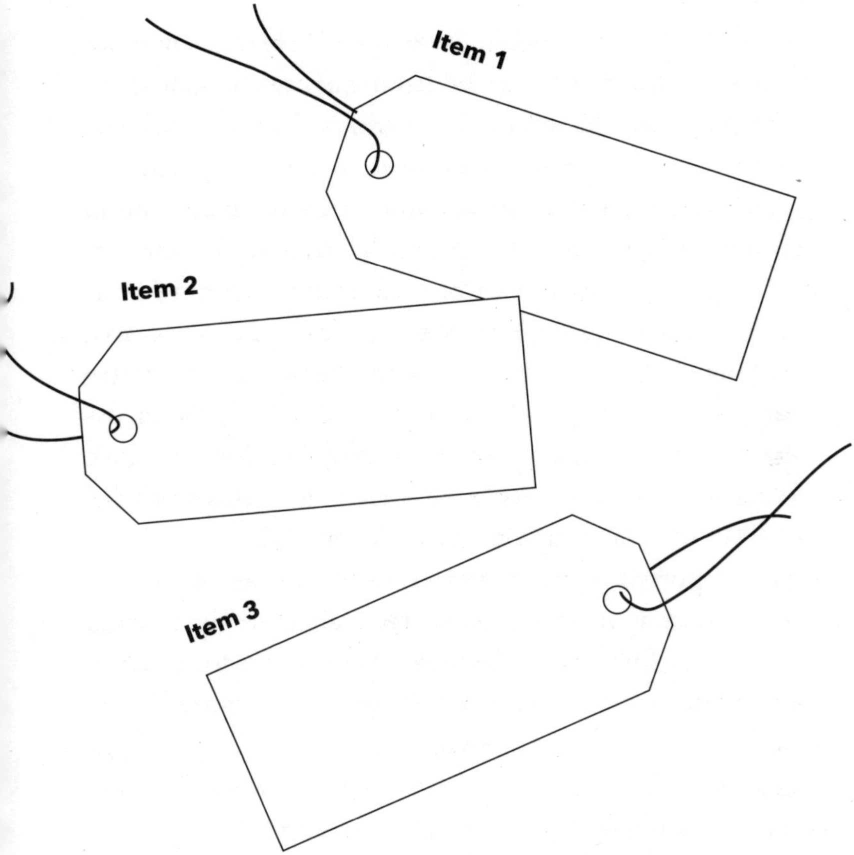

FASHION V. STYLE

Item 1

Item 2

Item 3

How likely do you think it is that you will keep this item as long as you possibly can?

When you have completed the task, you will have indicated whether or not your item of clothing retains its value to you, no matter what the current trend is. Obviously, I have no idea what you have marked, but I'm willing to bet that almost anyone who does this task will agree that when they've experienced owning and wearing something that was beautifully made, from quality raw materials, that piece will have greater longevity in their wardrobe and will give back so much more in terms of feelings of warmth, joy and contentment for far longer than multiple cheaper things that come and go so quickly.

This is an essential part of understanding the differentiation that I am going to make between fashion and style. Fashion is that which is currently trending, the shapes, colours and versions of things that are being shown and shared and copied all over magazines, social media videos and ads. Fashion is very fast-moving and items can fall in and out of fashion in a matter of weeks. This is reinforced and supported by major brands now constantly renewing collections, with some high street labels easily churning out twenty-four new collections a year (Zara, for example) and global online retailers spewing out as many as two thousand new items each week.[6]

Style is different. Style has nothing to do with what is currently popular; in fact, it can be opposed to what is currently considered 'fashionable'. You can be an extremely stylish person and not follow any of the current trends. Think about people who are fans of period clothing and who regularly wear vintage styles from the forties, like the Queen of Burlesque, Dita Von Teese, or Mod styles from the sixties; take the awesome historical tailor (and coincidentally, an ex-pupil of mine) Zack Pinsent, who hasn't worn a single piece of modern clothing since he was fourteen years old. These are stylish people. People with sartorial passion and verve. People who adore clothes and who weave their flair into their everyday lives. Their style may not be currently 'in fashion' but I am certain they would hold no desire to be considered so. These people have the unique ability to pull an outfit together, to get a balance and a blend. They know the exact way to draw the eye to certain details, a way to combine shapes, textures and colours harmoniously so that an 'outfit' is created rather than it being just 'things being worn'.

When something is made well it can transcend the micro-moment of fashion and become a real forever piece. It can become part of your life, and part of your own, highly personal style. I have a treasured woollen cardigan in rich autumnal colours that I bought in a charity shop a few years ago. After some research from the label, I understand that it was a hand-knitted, luxury line cardigan from the high-street shop Monsoon, and it was for sale in a collection that they ran in the eighties. Even back then, it was about £100 to buy new, which would have made it a very expensive item of clothing, but it's one which has lasted the past forty years. I love that cardigan and I wear it almost every evening in the flat like a sort of postmodern housecoat. Now, if ever I were to dump that cardigan in an odd location, to drape it over the back of a park bench, or hang it from a hook in a café, miles from home, and if ever my unaccompanied children were to stumble across it, they would instantly be struck with the knowledge that I was close by. This is because there is so much of me in that cardi, I have spent so many hours in it that it's like a part of me for those few who know me and see me at home. It's my style. If someone else were to wear it, the chant from these quarters would be, 'that's such a mum-style cardi'. I have no idea whether it could be called fashionable and I really don't care, but it is my style and I am happy to identify with it in that way. It feels warm and enveloping, its colours are my colours, the wool is strong but soft, it looks great on top of leggings, dresses, jeans, with a belt or without – it will keep going for years to come. It has style and it's *my* signature style in the same way that kilt pins have become my signature style tool. A kilt pin nipped into the right place can create a thousand different secure looks with the things you already have. Believe me and invest in one!

Task: My Signature Style

What about you? Can you pick one item that, if left draped over the back of a chair, would make people think you were near? What item defines you? What's your signature style?

FASHION V. STYLE

Add it to the chair, draw or write to describe the piece of clothing that would most identify as quintessentially you.

_____

_____

_____

_____

Task: Style Council

And here's a list for you to finish off – it's a list of people that I think are super-stylish, beyond current fashion, these people simply ooze style . . . Add some more names, add some people who you think should be there. They don't have to be famous – it could be your friend at work, your grandpa; there are just some people who 'have it':

Iris Apfel
Stephanie Yeboah
David Bowie
Bjork
Jean Woods
Harry Styles
The Artist (Formerly Known as Prince)
Noel Fielding

NOT NEEDING NEW

_____

_____

_____

_____

If I look at this, it's obvious that all of these individuals have one thing in common . . .

Confidence. These people do not hide away feeling awkward about what style choices they make. There's a massive amount of power in showing your confidence and in taking pleasure in what you're wearing. You will tell people what to think about your choices even if you don't say a word. For example, imagine that you put on a big puffy jumper that you love, but you're aware it's unusual and you then spend the majority of the day tugging away at it, trying to minimise its impact, trying not to be seen, trying to flatten it down. If you are trying to minimise it, then you are not going to be showing confidence. Other people will pick up your low energy and uncomfortable feeling and they will respond to that. If, however, you wore the same jumper and strode out, head held high and you 'told' the world that it was ACE and you loved it, then the chances are that people will feel drawn to you and your irresistible personal style. Frequently we dictate what other people think by showing them how to view it.

There is no way that all of the people on our combined lists of stylish humans would be considered to have similar taste or share matching outfits, so it's not simply that these people are wearing the 'right' things; they each have different styles but the unifying factor that makes them rank highly in our minds is the way that they present themselves to the world and offer up their choices with a certainty that makes other people believe in them.

We can all try to work a bit of this attitude into our existing wardrobes. As fashion is constantly shifting, it doesn't matter exactly what style clothes you have access to, as long as you have some that fit you well, you will be able to put them together and create looks that you will feel pleased with. As soon as you do, then start to believe in yourself and your choices. Tell yourself it looks good, hold yourself with pride, add that scarf, bag, hat or brooch and focus on feeling good in your clothes, feeling proud and good about what you've put together. Just go for one walk around the block where you keep a mantra in your mind, 'I feel good in this, this is my stylish choice'; smile, listen to yourself and enjoy a few moments of experiencing confidence. You might not truly believe it at first, but just try and see what it would feel like and build up from there. You deserve to feel good in the things that you like for yourself. If you can do that, it's half the style vibe conquered already. Like water flowing downhill, people like to take the easiest route to making a connection, and if you're showing that you're stylish in your attitude, that's what they will assume.

Looking after the clothes that you already own is a very important part of maintaining your style without constantly buying new items. This can be thought of in three main areas: washing, mending and storing.

If you manage to keep fewer, better clothes (which is entirely possible after you've had a sort out and stopped buying so much), you will have the space to really focus on caring for the good things that have made it through your edit. Below I will share a few pointers that have supported me in keeping some of my clothing for decades and some aspirational methods we could all think about trying.

Washing

I wash almost everything in the machine. I know that some items state hand wash only or dry-clean only, but I have taken the risk with almost everything. As a single working parent of two children with uniforms and sports kits, I just haven't had the time I would have liked to hand-wash clothes at the sink or the money to dry-clean things. I use the most basic own-brand supermarket powders in the cardboard boxes because they are the cheapest (I make more sustainable choices when funds allow and I've also tried ivy leaves, etc.) and I don't use fabric conditioner (though I do try to remember to use a monofilament bag to collect any micro-plastics). The most important thing is to remember to turn that temperature dial right down when washing anything that might be delicate. Over the years I have made those simple errors and been left with a child-size jumper that I would never be able to wear again. By taking care with items, we can ensure they stay in our wardrobes far longer.

Drying

I don't have a tumble dryer or any outside space where I could have a washing line – I don't even have any radiators in the flat – so everything must dry on an old-fashioned wooden rack called a Sheila-Maid, which hangs from a pulley in my stairwell. A dehumidifier whirs away in winter to help with this.

Now, although this is not the most convenient way to get the washing done, what it has done is saved my clothes from the harsh environment of the tumble dryer with all the heat and friction wear from the rotation, and spared it any weathering out there in the garden that I don't have! I'm sure this has helped to keep my items in good condition, so could be worth thinking about if you're able to keep your space well ventilated. Heated drying racks gain rave reviews and are inexpensive to run in comparison with tumble driers.

Ironing

The bane of all of our lives! Now if I'm being honest, I don't personally iron unless I have a job interview, though occasionally I will steam something if the creases are too awful. Having said that, I appreciate that ironing can be part of a ritual of caring for your clothes, and some people take deep satisfaction in using ironing to keep their things looking pristine for as long as possible – this is a very good thing! We all know how different a well-loved shirt can look when you've run an iron over it, rather than simply tugging at the creases and hoping for the best.

To level up your ironing even more, you can use a few drops of essential oil mixed with distilled water and some vodka in a spray bottle to refresh clothes between washes and keep things lasting for longer.

Stain Removal

I really recommend Nancy Birtwhistle's bestselling book *Clean and Green* for dozens of environmentally friendly and cost-effective household cleaning and laundry tips, including a host of recipes for stain removal.

A brilliant trick I have gleaned from Nancy is to keep a tub of percarbonate of soda at home. This is also known as 'oxygen bleach' or 'green bleach' and when used with hot water, it creates a stain-removing fizz of foam that is the most effective treatment I have ever used. It's virtually harmless when it enters the water system after use and it will get the nastiest of stains from the whitest cottons and linens.

Taking the time to remove those stains is so important. Often it will take far less time than you think and will stop you replacing a perfectly good piece of clothing. If you don't want to make up your own stain-removal solution, there are lots of great ones that can be bought, and they will be a lifesaver when that inevitable cup of coffee gets spilt!

Extra Care Accessories

I have also invested in a handheld de-bobbler for woollens and for synthetic sportswear (you can put the natural fibre lint outside for birds to use in nests). This occasional treat for your clothes will restore them to a state that looks quite new again. It's incredible what a difference can be made to the appearance of a jumper or jacket by 'shaving off' all of the snaggy bobbles of fibres caused by friction over time (known as pilling).

Reusable lint rollers or brushes are also a great investment; at one time I thought them to be rather outdated and perhaps the sort of thing that some elderly uncle might bring out to dust off some velvet blazer before an organ recital. Now, after years of wasting metres and metres of Sellotape in that 'wrap your hand backwards' technique of fluff removal, I can vouch for the acquisition of a decent lint remover in the home. It will, again, save you over-laundering your clothes.

Rewearing

The biggest factor in keeping my clothes looking vibrant and protecting them from wearing down has been that I do not automatically put them into the washing pile just because they have had one wear. This is a really important thing to stress. With the exception of knickers, underwear and socks, you do not have to wash your clothes each time they have been worn. You can be the judge of how frequently you do need to do it, but for most people who're not involved in manual labour, your trousers, skirts, pullovers and even shirts will not routinely be so dirty that they need to be sent through the washing system every night. If you get used to inspecting them, having a little scrumple-up and sniff, hanging them to air somewhere (outside or the bathroom during a steamy shower) and then wearing them again another day, you will be sparing your favourite things from excessive and unnecessary washing, sparing your wallet from expense on detergent, energy and new clothes, and supporting the environment through your lower power and resource usage. Win–win–win!

Storage

I have very limited storage space for clothes as I don't have my own bedroom and everything has to fit into a space which is essentially a small landing. I try to hang as many things as possible but also have tubs under my sleeping shelf for storing the smaller things, like underwear and tights. I have learnt that cotton pillowcases are very useful as you can use them to protect your woollens from the ravages of moth infestation. The larvae of clothes moths are the pesky things that will eat wool, fur, feathers – basically anything with keratin protein in. They will not, however, eat clean cotton as it's a plant fibre, so it can be a good idea to place your woolly items inside cotton pillowcases and roll them up safely as one line of defence against this very common pest.

Moths also dislike cedarwood oil and the practice of adding some drops of cedarwood essential oil to cheap vodka in a spray bottle to spritz over the things in your wardrobe is another good way to deter them from hanging around. You can also use the small cedarwood discs that pop over the metal hook of a coat hanger to infuse the scent too. These can be topped up every few months with a couple of booster drops of oil if you buy yourself a bottle.

Good storage and organisation is key to feeling content with enough. You need to be able to see what you already have so that you remain aware of all the things you don't need to buy again! If you have stuffed your drawers and cupboards with clothes that you're scrumpling up and ramming in, you will lose track of what there is and precious materials will be wasted. Clothes will not become clothing; they will simply be furniture-stuffing.

Mending

If you really want to get the most from your clothes, to keep them going as long as possible and to feel the true joy in owning something decent and looking after it, you will probably want to make sure that you have a basic knowledge of mending skills like learning to tack up a fallen hem, sew a button back on, close up a seam rip and attach a patch. It's incredibly rewarding to learn a little embroidery, and it will enable you to add personal touches to items that, as well as being decorative, can also cover up permanent stains or mend a hole.

And don't worry at all about not being skilled enough to carry out perfectly invisible mends yourself; firstly, there are a growing number of mending agencies and professionals who are available for business with their incredible skills; and secondly, basic visible mending is now seen as an outward sign of caring about sustainability and being committed to turning against the behemoth of disposable fashion – a bit of a badge of honour.

Styling What You Already Own

The whole reason that I first began Not Needing New as a social media account was because of the number of people who would comment on what I was wearing, and who would ask where I had bought something. It felt important to show other people, perhaps in the same economic squeeze as myself, that it was possible to still feel good, to feel stylish and most importantly, to not feel humiliated or irrelevant in terms of what clothes were available in second-hand places.

I began to document different ways to put together outfits on a budget, only using preloved items. It went down really well and I grew a real community of followers who were happy to see an ordinary woman wearing relatable things found in charity shops, in a way that they would be able to take useful ideas from.

I don't have a rule book, per se, and it's important to remember that you must do what makes you feel good, but in case you like having a few pointers of the ways in which I pull together the outfits that I show on @not.needing. new, here are a few really simple tips that I use daily when I'm deciding how to wear the clothes I already own:

Tight/Baggy

I like to think about the balance of my outfit as I am putting it together. I always make sure that if I'm wearing something baggy on my top or bottom half, I will wear something more fitted on the other. For example, if I am wearing a massive, oversized sweatshirt, I might pair it up with leggings. If I have a very tight clingy top, I wouldn't choose a pair of leggings because I would prefer to balance it with a flowing skirt or some fabulous floaty trousers. I think this works aesthetically based upon the golden thirds principle, a two-thirds/one-third idea about the balance that humans find most pleasing in art that we can relate to the way we dress. Things that cut you in half tend to draw the eye right to a middle point rather than the more comforting overall composition created by the golden thirds.

Layering

This is a such a huge part of good styling. It sounds ridiculously easy and some may think that it in no way warrants a whole section in any book – it's just wearing one thing on top of another thing, after all – we all do this. However, there *is* a subtle art to layering things in a thoughtful way that will showcase glimpses of texture, will allow your shape to sing out, and will gather a colour palette that brings you a really polished look. You need to build up a few key items to level up your layering game: a plain, tight round-neck T-shirt, plain long-sleeved T-shirts, light cotton shirts, a denim shirt, a cashmere jumper, a cardigan, a blazer and a decent coat.

If I have a long shirt, I like to layer it with a cropped jumper over the top and pull the sleeves down beyond the cuffs of the jumper, the shirt deliberately poking out rather than being tucked away and hidden.

I like waistcoats with long-sleeved tops or dresses underneath and I absolutely swear by the unbeatable warmth of having a cashmere layer next to your skin in the winter. Try experimenting with combinations that you have never tried before; I recently saw expert styler Caroline Jones (@knickers_models_own) putting a collared shirt on underneath a boiler suit and it looked amazing!

Colour/Pattern

Usually I won't combine more than two main 'base' colours in an outfit because having added all the other elements like earrings, a watch, the design on your trainers, etc., you're very likely adding in more sparks of colour anyway, and it may suddenly feel that there's too much going on.

With too broad a mix of main colours, the eye is drawn all over the place and the outfit may feel disjointed and odd.

Pattern clashing can work well as an amazing style statement but for it to look really good, it needs to have some sort of unifying element behind the choice. If the colours work together, they can carry off a proper big clash of pattern and look very intentional and spot on.

Colours should either contrast really well (think yellow and black, navy and cream) or be tonally friendly (muted teal and soft orange). Don't worry at all about which colours are 'in' – remember, when we get the December alert that Pantone have chosen the colour of the year for the following year and everyone starts buying hauls of that newly named shade, remind yourself that a panel of people have decided what this colour will be; it's not some word of the Almighty set into tablets of stone. It was chosen by some humans, no more important than you, and you are free to disregard it as much as you wish, and carry on with the colours you already love and own.

However, I do think there's some value in 'getting your colours done'. This is a service offered by personal stylists where you are matched with a set of shades and tones that best suit the whole combination of your skin tone, hair and eye colour. You sit in front of a mirror while a series of different coloured drapes are laid across your shoulders and you can witness the instant effect of the block colour against your own complexion. I think it can really help if you struggle to know what works well for you – it can be pricey but it's possible to book a consultant who will come to your home and do a group of friends all in one session, so you may be able to share the cost and have a fun evening of it. It may be worth the one-time spend as it will help you in knowing what you feel most confident in moving forward, potentially saving you from making fast-fashion choices that will end up being unloved and unworn.

Accessories

Edit your wardrobe so that you keep a really decent set of quality basics. You can work on treasure-hunting in charity shops to try to build up a collection of staples that you'd consider timeless (i.e. simple designs without labels or trendy details) – things like tailored trousers, a suit jacket, a black dress, a plain knit V-neck, a cashmere scarf, a floaty summer dress, a well-cut waistcoat. When you have a good basic wardrobe, you can create endless outfits by combining the base items and then playing around with accessories.

Silk scarves, belts, bags, brooches, coloured and textured tights, bangles, necklaces, hats – you can keep your outfits feeling exciting and fresh without buying new clothes, by looking through the amazing selection of accessories in almost every charity shop in the land.

I have a pair of fabulous statement beaded earrings that I wear over and over again; they are big and bold and they're covered with a detailed mosaic of neutral tones and golden glimpses. They were passed on to me after having been owned for over twenty years by my jeweller friend, Emma Stanton. These earrings have the ability to make one black dress, or simple jeans and T-shirt into an 'outfit'.

Platforms like Pinterest can be really useful to get fresh seasonal ideas for accessory combinations and you can use social media to serve you handy tips like scarf tying tutorials, but ultimately I advise you to unsubscribe and look away from screens when it comes to the mailing lists of the big fashion retailers. Opt out as soon as you can; having these 'friendly' emails sent directly to your inbox and commanding your attention creates a huge temptation to shop the enticing offers and the messaging will always be designed to make you feel as though you'll be missing out if you don't click through – you won't be.

Decent Shoes

Although you can sometimes get lucky and find really fantastic preloved footwear, I would suggest making sure that you have a really good, well-fitting pair of shoes that you know are not causing you any long-term damage by being incorrectly sized. It can be great fun to browse online preloved sites and charity shops to see what's on offer, and occasionally you will spot something wonderful when you need it – I actually found authentic blue suede baseball boots made by Gucci for my son once – but as it's critical to your overall health that you don't damage your feet, I think there is a great deal of wisdom and sustainability action in investing in well-made footwear and taking time to look after it. We have always had the tradition of cobblers in the high street, it's one area of mending that has

never fully left the public sphere and hidden itself away. Somehow, despite the radical obliteration of our 'make do and mending' habits since the Second World War, we have mostly managed to cling onto the shoe-menders and I hope we make more use of them. It's quite miraculous what can be done to preserve the life of boots and shoes by way of a new sole, new heel, repaired rip or a replaced zipper. If you do have a cobbler in your local town, pop in and ask about all the different services that they offer; they can usually fix coats and bags too as their sewing machines are strong enough to cope with folded leather and really heavy fabrics like canvas.

Of course, fashion can be fun and can feel really important to us all, who want to dress well and have pride in our appearance. As was mentioned at the start of the chapter, what you wear is likely to be the primary mechanism by which you are instantly accepted or judged in society. However, we know that our collective relationship to fashion has to change, with billions of petro-chemical-based fibre garments being slung into waste streams that are genuinely choking both deserts and seas; we need to turn the tide and select fewer, better items of clothing. We need to become the start of the change we wish to see, to become the solution.

We can have incredible and lasting style without dancing to the enforced beat of the industry where only billionaires are getting any lasting value. We can play our own, more fitting and more confident tune; we can embrace the things we truly love for much longer and we can seek the actual joy in building relationships and memories with the *actual* fabric of our lives.

CHAPTER 7

Health and Beauty

Another area of life in which we're inclined to fall for the temptation to buy it all, and to engage with the never-ending marketplace of continually evolving and reinvented offerings, is the world of health and beauty. According to data for the mid-2020s, the UK health and beauty market alone was worth over £30.4 billion in 2025 and is set to continue to increase at pace, currently growing four times faster than the rest of the economy.[1] There is an awful lot of stuff out there promising eternal youth and perfect health, and it comes at a cost.

It's no longer the sole preserve of women either; just as with Bernays' incredible marketing move with the cigarettes (as described in Chapter 4), cosmetic companies have realised that societal attitudes are shifting, allowing them to hook the male audience in, with what I guess will be largely the same ingredients in the same products, but in different packaging featuring slogans about how 'powerful' and 'strong' instead of how soft and sensitive it is, and convincing men how ruggedly good it feels to take care of yourself.

As products become ever more specific in their targeting, and available at the press of a button, the temptation to buy into the buzz around what they're going to offer for your hair, face (eyelashes, armpits, toes, décolletage, eyebrows . . .) becomes harder to resist. Especially hard when even our daily channels of communicating with friends are now peppered with ads making targeted claims due to algorithms gathering info about you. My children's generation are regularly treated to influencers showing hauls of cosmetic products in bedrooms which look, to the casual Gen X glancer anyway, like the shelves in a high street chemist's shop. Stacks of perfumes, rows of hair styling potions, drawers containing so many products that you could easily be mistaken for presuming the person was prepping to maintain a fully groomed aesthetic till the end of time.

Aside from the massive amount of money that we are collectively forking out on all of this stuff, there are a few other issues that we should be mindful of. The global organisation CleanHub, which was set up by two surfers in order to tackle plastic pollution in oceans and seas, reports that the beauty industry produces 120 billion items of packaging every year, 95 per cent of which is not recycled.[2] The numbers are staggering. The report on CleanHub's website goes on to suggest that in terms of self-reflection and analysis of internal data on waste, the beauty industry has been largely overlooked by the media in favour of a focus on fast fashion and food waste, and has not been doing enough of the work required to change systems and to create more sustainable pathways to products. Once again, that leaves us, the consumers, needing to make more careful decisions about what we want, not only for our bodies, but also for our environment. It makes it even more important to only buy what we need, and to choose what we are buying really well.

In this chapter I'll share my routines and chat you through some guidance for maximising access to really decent, evidence-backed health and beauty basics, with a slant on affordability and the consideration of the wider impact in terms of sustainability. There are so many tiny tweaks that can help you to break the habit of falling for every new health and beauty fad that you're pushed towards, and tips that can support you in feeling great about yourself now and into the future without spending huge amounts of money, or adding greatly to the heap of discarded packaging and half-used chemicals that we've been inadvertently amassing.

I will start with the real basics like sleep, water and nutrition. You can spend all the money you like on creams, gels, lotions and serums but if you're also chronically dehydrated, sleep-deprived and eating ultra-processed foods, you're going to be doing nothing more than firefighting at the very margins of the healthy glow you're trying to achieve. It's a hard one to sell as a 'top tip' because none of us really wants to hear this. We all know better and yet still look for a new cream to promise us the dewy, fresh skin of the adverts. It just shows how much we look to pay for a solution in order to keep going with the routine of our hectic lives, rather than having to dismantle all the props we rely upon to keep us pushing through. Late nights, too many wines, a high salt intake, traffic fumes, and offices with heating and air-con are factors that affect our well-being and complexion and we can go a long way towards counteracting them with the right basic hydration for our bodies.

I am not a beauty queen, not a model, film star or goddess

of any description, but I have been told that I have good skin 'for someone in their fifties' (we'll discuss the exhausting business of unavoidable and natural ageing later) and there is one major thing that I attribute it to. It's a highly unpopular thing to proffer as a suggestion: no alcohol.

I gave up all booze in May of the first UK lockdown in 2020. I had the deep realisation that in that global moment of change, the intensity of life in a small, high flat, without people, work or school routines and with my two young children to try to steer through the frightening loneliness and loss ahead, that I would end up drowning myself in red wine. I was already 'rewarding' myself nightly with Merlot, hiding bottles behind the cornflakes and feeling ashamed when the clanking glass recycling was all booze and not bolognese jars. It was making me tired, anxious, puffy, increasingly sick at the weekends, skint, snappy, dehydrated and overweight. It wasn't serving me at all, and yet I was giving it to myself as a reward for being a hard-working single mum who deserved to have it as a treat.

Anyway, despite not really wanting to end those lovely first relaxing sips of that comforting glass of red each night, in May 2020 I decided to see if I could do five weekdays without drinking in the evening, and I basically just haven't stopped stopping. I lost two stone in the first two years and feel better than I have for decades. It's annoying to hear anyone going on about how great they feel, so I will try not to bore you, but will simply say that there is no cream in the world that would have rejuvenated my skin in the way that giving up alcohol did, and no vitamin shake that could make me feel as good as I now do, daily. Not to mention the huge amount of money I saved. If you're drinking enough, the cost soon racks up and it was a revelation to see what cutting it out did to my bank balance.

Giving up alcohol may not be on your radar at all, but if you have ever felt that curiosity, that pull towards drinking less or not at all, all I can do is encourage you. It has improved every area of my life and I think you'll start seeing the benefits quickly too.

EATING WELL

In the health and beauty balance, I truly believe that what you're routinely putting into your body is of far more significance than anything you could rub in or dose up on. This is good news from a financial point of view as it's often about saying no to the spend on drinking, smoking or eating highly processed foods and embracing the more basic cheaper options. There will be a thousand adverts in the wellness arena offering you all manner of diets, supplements, protein powders and extracts in order for you to eat well, but in truth, you can do this for yourself by shopping for fresh vegetables and fruit, grains and rice, potatoes and eggs, fish and herbs – whatever dietary preferences you have, there will be options for you to buy your own ingredients and to make healthy, filling meals and snacks without needing to resort to pre-made, highly packaged and expensive options.

Often, our ultra-processed food habit is just our way of managing time. It's no wonder that we have been collectively choosing to buy stuff we can eat without needing half a day to prepare it; we are having to juggle so many demands in our lives in an era where almost every household needs at least two full-time earning adults to support the massive cost of housing. People just don't have the hours available to suddenly whip up a healthy, nutritious meal that everyone can pull a chair up to and enjoy, the minute they get home from work and hang their coat up. We need to give ourselves a break from the pressure to be brilliant at everything, but at the same time develop a new set of habits that fit in with the hectic lives we lead, which will support us in eating well.

This is going to look different for everyone; ethical and cultural practices as well as specific dietary requirements will dictate what's right for you, but in essence, forward planning is your saviour here. One of the most useful things I have done is to realise when I am most likely to reach for junk food for convenience and finding my own solution. I know it sounds ridiculously worthy of me, but for a couple of years I have been taking three raw carrots and two apples to work wrapped up in a tea towel in my bag. I always want to start snacking on something about 10.30–11 a.m., so being able to reach under my desk and pull these out (they are so good if you can coordinate eating them at the same time) has stopped me from taking any of the biscuits available in the workshop. It's routine now, it's just what I do on autopilot every day, and I enjoy it. I buy a bag of carrots every week, and it's so cheap and easy, the same as having a flask and making tea to take with me – it's habit and it means I am in control of exactly what I want to eat and I'm not drawn to making poor choices through having no alternative.

Investing in a good flask, tiffin tin or Tupperware tub, and having a ready supply of ordinary cotton tea towels is a great help in making sure that you have the tools to carry your own choice of food around.

Other ways to bring the Not Needing New mindset to eating well:

- Menu plan – I have to admit, I am NOT good at this, but I am trying! It's an amazing way to reduce waste, to avoid the 'I have no clue what's for dinner' days and to negate the last-minute overspend on takeaway suppers, be that supermarket-boxed or actually from a restaurant. Making a weekly list of main meal ideas before you head out to the shops is all you need to do. Just create it while you stand looking at what you already have to make sure you're not buying twice and to help you to use up what you already have in. There are so many chefs and foodies online who have created weekly meal plans for every dietary requirement, so you don't even have to do this work yourself. Just find one you like and go for it.

- Don't be afraid to eat the same thing over and over again. If you find a healthy and simple meal that you don't mind cooking after a long day at work, then feel free to repeat it as many times as you like. It's a good way to make sure you use up the usual ingredients it takes to make it, and means you aren't looking for new gadgets or hard to find ingredients every time you pick a recipe.

- Follow accounts that show you easy swaps that you can make while you are shopping so that you are able to identify the 'clean' versions of everyday products, free from unnecessary additives, extra oils, and sugars. Sophie Morris (@sophie_morris) is an excellent example of someone who offers this advice for free on her social media channels, and I am a big fan of the work of Kimberley Wilson (@foodandpsych), psychologist and author of *Unprocessed: How the Food We Eat Is Fuelling Our Mental Health Crisis*.

- When you are cooking a good meal using decent ingredients, make a little bit more than you're going to eat so that you can freeze a portion or two and have it in your freezer on standby for the days when you can't manage to cook. It's also possible to premix the dry ingredients for healthy family favourites such as lentil soup or savoury rice and store them in the cupboard until needed. Elly Curshen (@ellypear), who is a BBC food awards finalist and regular writer for the *Waitrose Food* magazine, shares many tips like this for using leftovers and for saving time and money while eating gorgeous, nutritious meals.

- Cut up some of your raw vegetables, like carrots, celery, peppers and cucumber, and store them stacked into some cool water in a mug or bowl in the fridge to pick on during the day. You'll eat them if they are ready and waiting, but you'll probably leave them waiting in the bottom fridge drawer if they're not. This is always what happens with kids and teenagers too – if you want them to eat something decent, just start chopping up raw veggies and they will appear as if from nowhere and start lifting them off your chopping board (which is pretty annoying when you're cooking, but use the same method to lure them in, and get them eating well).

- You can also freeze surplus fruit – berries and bananas (peel them first!) can go in raw, citrus in slices (great to add to drinks), cooked apples and pears and purees, etc., ready for pies and crumbles later in the year. I use a lot of my frozen bananas for making smoothies; I'll unpeel them and add them to the freezer when they have moved beyond my short window of tolerable ripeness for ordinary consumption.

- Freeze the ends of veg that you cut off (the tops and tails, the outer leaves) and keep them in a freezer bag until you have enough to make a decent veggie stock – just pop them into a pot with a lid, cover with water, add a bay leaf, a pinch of salt, and any other herbs you like and simmer away for a while. Strain it through a fine sieve and you have a great stock from the waste you were going to get rid of. All of the flavours from the scraps will be as good as the flavours from the 'good' bits.

- Make it a habit to occasionally go through your fridge and see if there are enough odd bits to make a soup or salad. Depending on the season, you're likely to have fresh produce, especially in that lower drawer, which gets dangerously close to being unloved. It can still be chopped up for a soup in a slow cooker, or chopped and grated into a lovely summery salad. Eating seasonally appropriate food is important for our own health, supporting us to have a variety of fresh foods with a richer diversity for our gut microbiomes throughout the year, and due to the lower food miles created by eating what's available nearby at any one point in the year, you're opting for a more globally sustainable way of eating.

I'm going to give you a recipe now – it's the food of gods to me. Honestly, if I had to choose just one meal to eat on repeat for the rest of my days, this is the one. Gus, my long-time builder-boyfriend and a life-long vegetarian himself, cooks this for me and ignited my love for it. I'm sharing it with you because it's cheap, fresh, suitable for vegans, vegetarians, pescatarians and omnivores, it's gluten-free, it can be dairy-free and it keeps for a few days in the fridge. It's basically perfect for almost everyone. It's Gus's Dal – make a batch of it and make extra for the freezer.

These are the ingredients that we used to feed the two of us (with leftovers to eat for breakfast and beyond) when I recorded the process, but all the veggie options are interchangeable according to what you like:

NOT NEEDING NEW

Ingredients
1 brown onion, diced
Salt
250g red lentils
140g brown basmati rice
2 tablespoons curry powder/paste (to taste)
2 sticks of celery, chopped
1 sweet potato, diced
1 bell pepper (any colour), chopped
A little box of mushrooms
About 750ml stock
A head of pak choi
Coriander, to taste
Lemon or lime / yoghurt / pickles as condiments
You'll need two pans; a glass-lidded pan is best for the rice.

Method
- Chop up an onion and fry on low heat until translucent
- Add pinch of salt to help the onion sweat off
- Add your curry powder or paste of choice, and cook off for about 10 minutes. Stir to ensure there's no burning
- Cook your rice at the same time. Brown basmati is delicious. We always cover the rice with about two fingers of water above the rice in the pan, then bring the rice to the boil and let it simmer. After 2 minutes, turn off the heat and let it just sit with the PAN LID ON for the next 20 minutes. A pan with a glass lid is best for this
- Back to the dal – add the celery, sweet potato and bell pepper, and fry off for a few more minutes

HEALTH AND BEAUTY

- Add the mushrooms
- Tip in the red lentils
- Add stock (we used a mushroom stock cube and water), enough to make it feel like a very thick soup – it will seem like a lot of water but the lentils will soak it up (3:1 water to lentil ratio)
- Bring to the boil, turn down and simmer, stirring occasionally. Keep the lid on the dal and allow the whole thing to cook through. Keep a check on the water level; don't let it dry and burn. If the dal looks creamy but the lentils are hard, add more water and keep cooking
- Add chopped pak choi, and/or fresh coriander right at the end. Add a squeeze of lemon or lime
- Serve the dal with the cooked rice, and naan, pickles, yoghurt, etc. (as you wish)

HYDRATION

So much is said these days about the hyper-importance of good hydration, the correct electrolytes and the quest for the perfect almost surgically attached water bottle. I feel that it's a miracle that us Gen Xers, and earlier folk, are even alive. No one constantly imbibed water when we were young; we didn't even take it out on hot summer walks. We just stopped at a pub on the way home. No cars had drinks holders; they had cigarette lighters and ashtrays instead.

It seems we've moved on a bit! It's no doubt a good thing to have a bit of water now and again through the day, so I'm going to add it in here as a reminder. You don't need fancy bottles though; one of the best travel water bottles I use was originally a jar of Italian tomato sauce, a lovely-sized glass container with a sturdy reusable screw-on lid. While websites would sell me a fashionable 'plastic-free' glass drinking bottle for around £20, this one was £2 and it came with free tomatoes. All I had to do was wash it out after we'd eaten them.

BEAUTY

Right, so you're drinking water and eating more good, fresh stuff. That's the basic foundations laid already. From this starting point, you can trust that whatever skincare and cosmetics you buy aren't trying to work against the tricky conditions of incomplete nutrition and an exhausted liver.

The first big thing to say about 'beauty' in general is this: it is basically nonsense. Each generation is given a new beauty standard to meet, and then, through media and advertising, we are all trained in learning how to fake it to make it look like we naturally look like that. Thankfully the desire to adhere to the standards starts wearing off as you get older, I promise you that.

Beauty is for you to judge and no one else. Feeling at

ease with who you are, dressing for yourself, building routines that support your personal happiness, and not changing your appearance for others – that is beauty, and you will feel properly beautiful if you can get to that point, but it's hard. Everything we talk about in this book is going to help you get closer to that place – free of others' expectations and more deeply connected to your own standards and wishes.

SIMPLE BEAUTY HACKS

There are a few, very simple ways that I have managed to tag along with the 'beauty' expectations of my generation that I feel good about, but that do not demand that I spend loads of money on new stuff (and I know . . . in adhering to any expectation, I am being part of the culture and therefore the problems), but I do enjoy this element of self-care without getting drawn into fad after fad in an endless quest for perfection. This is all very basic stuff, but it works – I have tried thousands of products in my fifty-something years so far, and I have happily settled with a very low-key, low-cost routine that still manages to serve me well enough to get the occasional compliment about being 'glowy' and 'fresh'. Here's how:

Cleansing
Have a stack of dedicated face cloths by the basin. You can get a fantastically clean face at bedtime, which is important, with nothing more than warm water and a cloth. You need to clear your skin of the oils, pollutants and dead skin

cells of the day as these can possibly create stress responses in the skin and will certainly give you a dull layer of dry skin if not gently wiped away. You do not need soap products or expensive cleansers every night. You will probably want to have a deep cleanse and exfoliation from time to time, which actually, you can do really well with many waste food items (coffee grounds and mashed avocado, for example) but generally, if you have a shower every day and are washing your face well while you're in there, a simple pre-bedtime warm cloth wipe will lift any dirt and won't be adding unnecessary chemicals to your skin or to the water system. If you have eye make-up that's hard to shift, I absolutely swear by The Body Shop's Chamomile Cleanser in a tin, but you can also use supermarket coconut oil – it's not as easy to use but it's cheaper and if it's good enough to eat, it will not be damaging your complexion.

Moisturising

I have always loved face creams and moisturisers and have probably tried as many as I've had hot dinners. I tend now to keep one in the bathroom for post-flannel dewiness, one where I put my make up on (Instagram friends will know where this is!) and have one in my bag for emergency lizard-face situations. I have tried the fanciest of fancy creams: that La Mer stuff (via a swanky friend), the Lush 'Gorgeous' recipe (made for Princess Diana – smells divine due to the orange blossom) and some of the Clarins ones that they hand out to business-class passengers on flights (again, obviously not given to me directly). In all honesty, I have never truly seen that more money buys you better results. The one I have gone back to time and time again and will always want to have by my side is Weleda Skin Food, mid-price (more than Nivea, less than Clarins), a cruelty-free, biodynamic and organic preparation with Demeter standard soil regeneration at the heart of its creation. It's the most unctuous and wondrous of any cream I've tried, and I adore it. Personally, I do also use a sunblock as I am very fair-skinned and have been advised to do so between April and October (at the minimum), by an NHS consultant dermatologist. I use a mineral-based one from UpCircle, a company that creates products using the natural waste ingredients of the food industry.

Just remember to sweep your hands up when putting that moisturiser on. Spending a few minutes a day dragging your skin down when you apply creams and oils is a literal DRAG, so apply your product in upward movements and have a go at playing gravity at its own game. This is not science-backed research, it's just my thought process, but as I spend two sessions a day sweeping my skin with moisturiser or face oil, the lovely lifted and massaged feeling that comes from counteracting gravity helps me to feel that I don't need to buy into any special gadgets or book 'tweakment' sessions to do a similar thing for my skin.

Hands First

As you get older, your skin gets drier. If, like me, you started with dry skin anyway, you may well be almost reptilian by this point. I am in that boat. The trick, I have learnt, with moisturisers, is that because you tend to use a better, more refined and delicate one on your face than the one you slather on your hands, if you don't moisturise your hands before you try to do your face, the hands will soak up much of the good, and likely, more expensive stuff as you try to get it up to your face, and you'll use it up very quickly. My top tip is to have a less expensive hand cream around (the coconut oil I mentioned earlier being perfect here) to give your digits a quick top-up of their own before you use them to get your best cream onto your face and neck.

Cut It Up

Very simple, and I am sure we all do this, but in case it needs mentioning again, anything that comes in a tube can be eked out for days if you cut the tube with scissors and use what would have been trapped inside before you wash and hopefully recycle the packaging. On this note, reusable products of all sorts are a fantastic way to use less: face cloths, period pants and moon cups, old-fashioned razors with replaceable blades. More sustainable versions of our favourite products are coming back into the general offering and it's great to see that these are no longer so hard to find.

Multi-use Products

As far as make-up goes, there are some products which are capable of working very hard for you and performing more than one function. For example, I have a £5 tin of Revolution London rosy-coloured 'balm', which I use as a blusher to add a sheen of freshness to the duller wintery-skin days, as well as working brilliantly as a lip balm and surprisingly, it makes a great colour for eyes too – just dabbing the last traces of the product from your finger-tips onto the outer edge of the closed eye brings a flush of definition and a 'finished' look. I have even made my own rosy-coloured balms by heating up plain shea butter, coconut oil, and adding in the stumps of any lipstick on its last legs until I have a pleasantly pinky gloop which, if poured into a cleaned out and recycled cosmetic tin, will cool and set, and can become your new all-round product. (If you do buy make-up, I can tell you that supermarket stuff, particularly the Aldi/Lidl cruelty-free, vegan ranges by Lacura, is every bit as good as anything I've ever used and is so much cheaper than comparable brands. Just aim to recycle what packaging you can.)

On the subject of multi-use, don't forget that if you use shampoo, you can use the lather of it to wash the rest of your body in the shower – you do not need another bottle of anything to have another load of lather from as both products contain surfactants and water. Using shampoo as body wash works pretty well, but body wash as shampoo is a little less successful due to the specific negatively charged chemical molecules in hair products which are designed to cling to the hair shaft and make brushing easier. You may end up with a wilder tangle to tame after the towel if you use the body wash on your hair.

Bar it!

Having said that you can use shampoo foam instead of shower gel, I will now beg you to give up shower gel anyway. If you are able to, using bars of soap instead of plastic bottles of shower gel is something we need to get back to. Given that the average UK household uses 24 bottles of shampoo in a year, and we generally use shower gel at the same rate or more frequently than specific hair products, let's say an average UK household also uses 24 bottles of shower gel a year, and there are roughly 30

NOT NEEDING NEW

million households – that's 720 million plastic bottles from the UK alone just for our shower gel usage, something that we didn't even start using until the eighties.³ Before that, we all had bars of soap and they were absolutely fine. A bar of soap leaves no plastic behind, nothing needing the energy of recycling or, far worse, the impact of landfill, and there are some incredible small soap makers out there. See if you can find one at a local market and fall back in love with simple soap.

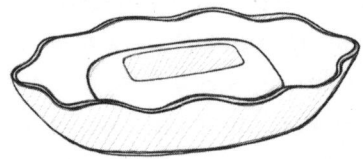

There is something so gratifying about paring everything back to the fewest, most simple things that you need to feel good. To help you to recognise this, I want you to think about beautiful bathrooms and how they make you feel.

Think about the nicest bathroom you've ever been able to get ready in, or the most luxurious bathroom you've seen in a magazine, the ultimate space for your self-care routine. I expect that you will imagine somewhere free of clutter, a place where there are only a very few, perfectly chosen products for use. Think of the feeling you get when you step into a really good hotel bathroom for the first time; you see that there is everything you'll need and there's space to breathe and to be. We don't need, or want, cupboards packed with tens of bottles of similar things, we don't need to buy into every new offering in order to keep up. It actually feels very liberating and grounding to make decisions about what you genuinely like, which brands you want to align with and which products are your heroes. When you settle for these, you can dial down all the clamour to have the next thing and you can relax into a long relationship with your signature things. It all feels calmer and infinitely more elegant.

AGEING

I want to take a brief moment here to talk about the anti-ageing aspect of the health and beauty market. We all know that it's big business, it's massive. We recognise the pseudo-scientific terms banded at us through television adverts in an attempt to sound authoritative: 'Derma-Restore, Rexaline Concentree, Peptide Retinol Moisture Balance Formula' blah, blah blah. Somehow all the cosmeceutical words make us think that it's a medical imperative that we have these products in our fight against the awful ravages of time – but again, it's mostly nonsense.

If you're going to be a more contented human, happier living away from the mania of non-stop consumption, then you will probably need to dig deep and find a way to feel confident in allowing your body to be what your body is. If you are fifty-five, you will not look twenty-five. If you are seventy-five, you will not look fifty-five. All of this is fine. It's wonderful, it's natural, it's beautiful and honest and true. Although you might fear looking eighty when you're forty, by the time you are eighty it will be perfectly, wonderfully right. The time, money, fear, self-loathing and trickery that you will leave behind if you allow yourself little steps towards accepting that time passes and things change, will be grounding and good.

I'm not suggesting you ditch all your products and the things that you enjoy about your personal care routines, but from experience, gradually shedding the fear of those physical changes has been a really welcome relief after a lifetime of being conditioned to believe that only youth is beautiful and acceptable.

I remember a time when my builder boyfriend was kneeling on the floor, probably plumbing in my dishwasher or something useful, and his daughter caught sight of the top of his head for the first time since she'd been carried on his shoulders, and she said, 'Dad! You're getting thin on top!', to which I immediately tried to diffuse the pain I imagined he'd be feeling, by saying, 'Don't worry, I'll still love you.' His reaction then caught me completely off guard and taught me something important. He sat back up and confidently remarked that he hadn't been worried at all about hair, and he hadn't thought for a moment that I wouldn't love him without hair, because why would you stop loving someone you loved over something so inconsequential as hair? He just couldn't understand what I even meant by that response. Of course, there is some male privilege we can acknowledge here, but ultimately it was a good reset about not automatically tying feelings of worth and value to looks.

I've thought about this moment and what it gave me. It offered an understanding that my own worth in a relationship isn't based upon how I look at any point in time, or how many products I wade through in a King Canute-esque attempt to hold back the seas of time; rather, it's based upon the massive tapestry of support, friendship and intimacy that we have treasured for all the years we have hung out together. You can't lose that, even if you can lose hair, or collagen, or a flat stomach.

Remember that.

SLEEP

Moving on, we may not all need or want make-up, but we do all need sleep.

The minimum amount of sleep we need in order for us to feel truly well will differ slightly from person to person, but official suggestions always seem to hover around the seven-to-eight-hour mark. 'Sleep hygiene' is a term which has crept into our parlance in the last decade and brings with it images of decent bedding, dark rooms and phone-free preparation time before bed, including lavender-scented baths and nineties non-Apple alarm clocks. Now I don't know anyone whose 'sleep hygiene' is quite this perfect, but doing what you can to support a good night's sleep is a really good way to support your own feelings of well-being.

You do not need a book to tell you that you need to get enough sleep. People will have been telling you this since back in the days when you were being tucked into your sheets with your teddy; children long to stay up late to be like adults, and many adults long to go to bed earlier! Good sleep is going to help you to regulate stress, control your emotional responses and mood, it will improve your cognitive functioning, and it can even support your immune system in fighting off illness and disease.

As busy people, we need plenty of sleep to keep things ticking over, but when we have so much to juggle, the brief opportunity for wind-down time at the end of the day is vital. As a result, we stay up much later than we should, in order to give ourselves some sort of run-off from the tasks and responsibilities of work, parenthood, our own parents and our household tasks. We end up staying up late and entering the 'scrolling danger zone'. You know the one where you're curled up on the sofa, TV series half interesting you, drink in one hand and phone in the other, thinking about what wonderful little things you could order that would make life seem a little less stressful and would make us feel a bit happier. These are when my most questionable shopping habits start to rear their ugly heads and I wish I had just gone to bed a little earlier.

Task: Reward Yourself with an Early Night

If we can't stay up late and order treats, I have another way for us to get that buzz of reward. Here's an adult reward chart for you. It may not have a sticker at the end, but it has an actual reward that you can tick off and colour in and feel good about. I am going to personally challenge you to go to bed earlier than usual on five nights over the next month. For arguments sake, let's make it 9.30 p.m. That is the challenge. Roughly one day a week. I want you to see if you can build this into your life for two reasons: you will feel better the more frequently that you can do this, and it will prevent you from doom scrolling or watching TV with ads popping into your world.

Make a plan to have that optimal sleep hygiene. Treat yourself to a bath or shower, have clean sheets that night, make sure you have a good book on the go, make sure your little bedside light is working and that you are warm and cosy enough. Leave your phone to charge in another room. Set an old-fashioned alarm, or make sure you have a means to wake up without that smart phone. This is not a punishment, this is a treat, so try to keep repeating that to yourself as you prepare to get into bed earlier, allow your body and brain to unwind and to enjoy the earlier night. As my rather eccentric dad always used to say to me, 'Early to bed, early to rise; makes a girl healthy, wealthy and wise.'

Day	What time did you go to sleep?	How many hours' sleep did you get?	Sleep quality rating out of 10?	How do you feel?
1				
2				
3				
4				
5				

EXERCISE

I can't write a chapter on health and beauty and not mention exercise in some form. Again, it can only be a layperson's guide coming from me, but there are simple ways to build in a base of movement which will maximise your daily opportunities for staying flexible and strong, as well as giving you the myriad benefits to mental well-being that exercise is known to offer.

As I mentioned at the beginning of the book, in the mass automation of tasks that's taken place over the last few decades, we've cut out a lot of the physical work of daily life; all of the machines that we love and live among have diminished the physical demands of our day and given us more time, which we've filled with work of other kinds, generally more sedentary work.

I'm not going to tell you to join a gym, or take up a particular sport, although those are great things to do; I'm simply not experienced enough to give you advice here. I had a brief period as a gym go-er in 1998 in Portugal when a swanky new David Lloyd gym opened near to Cascais, where I lived, and I was a single, full-time professional with no dependants, with access to spare money. I loved being a member, but I never broke out in a sweat; in fact, all I did was swim up and down the lovely pool with my head right up keeping a bun of dry hair and chatting to my friend about life, love and the universe as we drifted down the slow lane together.

The small ways that I (as a non-disabled person) stay active now include:

HEALTH AND BEAUTY

- Walking the dog three times a day, every single day.

- Walking locally whenever possible for shopping, etc.

- Carrying heavy food shopping bags up the stairs to the flat every week.

- Walking up and down the many flat stairs every single time I go outside for anything.

- Taking stairs and not lifts or escalators whenever possible.

- Being playful – still running about, jumping onto logs, ducking under branches, climbing over stiles, swimming in the sea, rolling down hills, trying to cartwheel still – anything to keep the body moving.

- Carrying and hanging out washing onto the pulley-dryer rack and hauling it up and down.

Keep in mind that you are made to move and try to keep building it into your life in small ways. Tiny changes over time will add up to a great difference. Walking and running are free, don't forget. Clambering about in the park and sea swimming are free too. Cycling is very inexpensive after the initial cost of the bike and absolute bargain bicycles can be found on local selling sites and even through police station auctions at times.

There are many brilliant ways to move and keep healthy without needing loads of expensive equipment and subscriptions, but it would seem that we're as addicted to buying stuff for sports as we are any other aspect of our consumerist lives. The UK sports and outdoor equipment market is currently worth around £12 billion a year[4] and with an estimated 10 per cent of that spend remaining completely unused, according to a survey of 2000 households by preloved selling platform Gumtree.[5]

They concluded that at least £1.5 billion worth of exercise gear sits in UK houses doing nothing more than gathering dust, having been bought in a wave of enthusiasm that didn't translate to routine change, or where they were tried once and simply were not the right fit.

The rapidly evolving market and the speed at which new designs and innovations are launched can leave the beginner feeling embarrassed about being seen with 'old' or 'basic' equipment and is often a real barrier to the likelihood of some people getting involved in sports and movement.

This crazy 10 per cent unused equipment figure does, however, highlight the enormous opportunity to search the second-hand market first if you're going to buy yourself any gear. At the time of writing this, a quick eBay UK search for 'used sporting goods' raised 130,000 items live and for sale, everything from yoga mats and horse bridles to ice hockey sticks and scuba masks.

There are activities that will cost nothing, but when stuff is needed, there are ways to save masses of money and reduce the further production of unnecessary products by heading for nearly new as your first port of call.

HEALTH AND BEAUTY

The health and beauty markets are enormous, they are powerful, and they have the ability to grab our attention really quickly. It's natural to want to find ways to become, and to remain, as well as we possibly can be, and any new offering which seems to have been created to do just that, is going to be of interest. We are glad to be given the tools to make the most of our bodies and our lives.

Just be mindful of the fact that it IS big business, that beauty corporations need your money in order to exist more than you need them in order for you to exist.

CHAPTER 8

High Days and Holidays

Not Needing New is not about losing ourselves in frugal misery. It's about finding a path through the unnecessary, it's about avoiding waste, reducing the expensive clutter that isn't serving you, and feeling content with all that you already have. In many ways you are going to feel better than you ever did before. There will still be fun times. There will still be high days and holidays.

But how to approach them?

What we will do in this chapter is firstly have a look at those big celebration days in our homes and share some ideas about how to enjoy a good time without feeling rinsed by commercialism, and then dive into our longer 'away' holidays and try to see a few ways to fling ourselves into the joy without tipping into stress over the costs and wider impacts.

When we think about excessive consumption and how this can affect us, it has been useful to use the idea of eating more than we need. This is an easy-to-understand starting point and one that we looked into early on in Chapter 2 because we have probably all done it at some time, and, using it as a template for considering the effects of having too much of a good thing is a relatable concept. When we try to remember this feeling of overindulging, it's likely that we will think back to our family celebrations and holidays. These are the times in the calendar that we break from the norm and we gorge. We binge until we're uncomfortable. We feast! We blow the food budgets on making the days as special as can be, for ourselves and for the other people in our circles.

We need to have these feasty moments pinned into our seasonal rhythm; it's a lovely thing to have a small part of the year where we allow the treats in. This is an important experience of being a human in a family, in a society, and in being part of a wider culture. Being here, in a Not Needing New mindset and living with a more contented foundation doesn't mean that it has to stop. We can find a way to enjoy celebrations without pushing ourselves into the negatives of excess that leave us broke, bloated and abashed. We do not need to wear ourselves out with the pressure to be gifting, decorating, and dressing up with new variations of the same things year after year.

What I remember most fondly from childhood about my family's Christmases past, in our crazy house full of children, wasn't anything to do with the things we optimistically circled in the Argos catalogue, it was to do with the magic that seemed to come from almost nowhere. The magic of Christmas Eve's sleepless expectation when Mum or Dad would walk around the house banging a wooden spoon onto a pan, while an older sibling told us to 'Shhhh, listen!' The belief that we could hear Father Christmas's sleigh rushing past overhead and because we were still awake, the sparkle of excitement knowing he'd whizzed off, away around the globe, and we must get to sleep so that our turn would come.

NOT NEEDING NEW

We would wake to the feeling of something being there, a weight on top of our feet, and I cannot describe how exciting that was, lying there in the winter darkness, yellow light from the landing slicing in under the door. The night before, we would go through our ordinary sock drawer and find a good, long knee-length sock to leave out for Father Christmas. We always got the same things in it: a satsuma, an apple, a balloon to blow up, a few pieces of chocolate money and a little toy. I can still hear the rustle, the crinkle of the unknown toy moving in the half-stuffed and knotted sock as we delighted ourselves by wriggling our toes slightly, holding back from sitting up and breaking the dream into reality, holding back for just long enough to let it still seem part of the beautiful night where prickles of magic fizzed into the house.

Downstairs the tree would be surrounded by presents, not because any one of us got loads, but because there were loads of us. No one was allowed to open anything until everyone got up, got dressed and had some breakfast. Our parents had to get the dinner started, get that turkey in and the pudding on to steam up the glass in the back door, and then it could start.

Ready with a pen and paper, Mum and Dad started the opening by inviting the youngest child to find a present with their name on. We all gathered round to see what they'd got, and Mum would write what it was on the piece of paper. The list that our parents made was essential as it was the only hope they had of being able to remember which of us had received what from whom, and then have any chance of being able to thank the right person for their kindness. We went around, one gift each, from the youngest to the oldest, to Mum and Dad, and back to the baby again. One at a time, opening each thing with the room watching, with the others looking ahead through the pile and finding a present for the next person. There was no frenzy of ripping paper, no pillowcases filled with stuff, it was an unusually structured ritual in our otherwise fairly wild household and it was just lovely. We appreciated the structure, I think. We liked knowing how this was going to be done and how it felt safe and predictable for us, something we will discuss in the parenting chapter later.

In all of the years of having Christmas with my troop of siblings, I don't think I remember what any of the tree presents were – except perhaps the year that I got a soft toy Snoopy? What I do remember with total clarity is one of the stocking-filler toys. One year we had tin sparking friction wheels, little hand-held spinners that whizzed a flint across rough metal and created arcs of sparks that flew out from the coloured plastic film windows to look like jolly red and blue fireworks. We sat in our bunkbeds, striking the sparks into the dark, the dangerous gunpowder-y smell of the burning flint adding to the magic.

We also had a paper advent calendar that hung on the wall by our coats. Tiny perforated card doors were ripped off if you were careless, behind which a picture lay. It was always the type of calendar with an individual picture – a robin, a bell, a gift, a lantern – it was never the fancy sort where each picture built a whole tableau and it certainly was never a chocolate calendar, for that was the stuff of a madman's dream! It would never have lasted anyway; I can't imagine the arguments. As it was, we took turns to open the doors of the paper one. There were probably five of us at any time who were in the appropriate age-zone to be able or interested enough to open the doors, and with twenty-four of them available, it meant that you would get four or five chances a year to be the one who saw the drawing first and called out to the others in the kitchen what it was that day. Somehow this was enough. It was enough because it was a special thing to do and there was nothing else to compare it with; we did not feel that other people had more or that we should be having more than we did.

Another family event that has gone down in our shared history book was the birthday party when there were so many of us around the table, that even with the benches that we had instead of chairs, there was just not enough room for all of us to eat at the same time. We weren't a family who always had to sit and eat together, but it would have been unheard of for us to not be together, around that big wooden kitchen table, on birthdays. The thought of some of us having to be in a different room was just too awful. Who would be left out?

A novel solution was found. We had an odd 'laundry' room with a reinforced glass sloped roof, a big sink and the two washing machines in. It was also home to the guinea-pig hutch where Smith and Jones, the squeaking piggies, were abiding in their hay-strewn home. The whole hutch was carried into the kitchen, placed alongside the table and swiftly covered in a cotton tablecloth. It was a bit rickety, a bit squeaky, and there was a distinct aroma of small rodent if you put your head down too low, but it was a solution and we were all able to eat together, the smallest kids delighting in having their special meal from the top of the guinea-pig hutch. So far from perfection from some perspectives, but actually completely perfect in the making of everlasting family memories.

Task: Celebration Memories

I have talked about a couple of celebration memories that really stand out for me when I think back to the years that I was growing up and living with my family. The parts that hold the deepest emotional weight were not the parts that could have been supplied by a shop. I wonder, for you, if there are things that you can pull out of your memory that feel similarly important? Take a minute to think back to times that you spent with the people in your childhood home. What are your favourite memories of family celebrations?

Now, see if you can place your ideas into these different areas:

```
Material objects I remember



```

NOT NEEDING NEW

Customs and traditions I remember

What I learnt from these experiences

The elements I will continue to enjoy

I wonder if there's anything to notice about how much of what was, and still is, important to you that comes from the material objects that you remember, and how much depended more on a shared experience?

It's neither depressing nor miserly to pull back a little from the excesses that are now seen as being the norm for big celebrations. It's important to remind ourselves that there were festivals we all enjoyed before there were adverts, before there was internet shopping, before Black Friday and before social media showed us the 'perfect' snippets of other families' days. If it all feels slightly out of control now, remember that you can decide to take back some of the control and you can place some limits to help get you through the good times without the uneasy feeling that it was all too much.

What we're supposed to be doing in these holiday times is breathing out, taking a break from the working rhythm of the year and trying to share symbols of love and connection with our community, be that our family or the wider realm of people who weave the fabric of our daily lives. These feast points are an essential respite for humans and for thousands of years we have behaved in this way. In the English county of Dorset, archaeologists have discovered evidence that leads to the strong conclusion that humans have been getting together to celebrate together for millennia. Barrow mounds have been discovered holding the remains of multiple cattle, all slaughtered at the same age, as identified by the wear to their teeth, which both ages the animals and dates their endings at a seasonal point, and shows us that humans were holding annual feasts to eat together as communities over six thousand years ago. Similar discoveries of animal remains indicative of feasting have been found in Galilee, again suggesting that the same communal gatherings were happening twice as far back in our human history, 12,000 years ago, before the advent of agriculture. It's likely that as populations grew and humans were forced to live in closer proximity, sharing their spaces, that group feasts were a way of cementing relationships where there may have been conflicts, and of strengthening bonds to forge a more resilient community in a harsher landscape.

So there really is a huge history in our practice of coming together to celebrate and share. It's in our nature and, still to this day, the sharing of resources and skills as we organise our parties and gatherings acts as a thread to weave us into stronger, more understanding families and community groups.

There do not have to be any hard or fast rules about how you manage your celebratory high days and we will all have very different ideas about the non-negotiable elements of what constitutes a holiday, whether that be a trip away or a festival day of celebration at home, but sometimes it's important to set some boundaries so that neither the burden of work nor cost falls too heavily for one person to manage.

For some of us, the annual big family celebration events do not equate to blissful moments of breathing out and coming together. For many of us, these 'high days' are actually more stressful than our ordinary working rhythms and they can lead us to spend weeks in advance worrying about how we are going to manage the pressure of delivering the 'perfect' event for everyone around us. It's not uncommon to rack up debts that take the rest of the year and beyond to try to manage or pay off, and this changes what is meant to be a time of loving togetherness, into a period that people can begin to dread.

There are a couple of key things that we need to remember – that communal feasting and celebrating was always done in a group, as a community. It was a shared event and it wasn't the job of one person to arrange every aspect for all of the others. In the developed world, many of us have simply fallen into a pattern whereby hosting the significant 'feast' of the year does fall upon the shoulders of one person, and often one who is also juggling working and looking after other generations. For the purpose of this section, I have written about Christmas and birthdays, but these are not the only family celebrations that fit the model of a significant festivity, and you may substitute it for whichever gathering best fits your community and family. Christmas adverts depict families with matching pyjamas, roaring fires, loaded platters, professional-looking cocktails in frosted glasses, tables bedecked with tasteful decorations, a perfect playlist and a huge pile of beautifully wrapped gifts. It's simply unrealistic for us to try to emulate these high-budget ads in our own houses every year.

We also don't have to try to make everyone's dreams come true. This is a vital piece of info. It is not your responsibility to make the festival perfect for everyone at the expense of your own financial and emotional well-being.

Gifting

Now let's focus on gifting.

We can't fill every gap for every person, gifting them all they dream of and ensuring that magic reigns from the start of any festival's countdown right through into the new season beyond. What we can do, however, is show gratitude and love to our closest people by giving them a little something to show that we love them; perhaps you will choose exciting new toys for the younger people in your circle, but for many others it's perfectly OK to look for a second-hand book about something that they love, find a fancy soap in their favourite scent, print out a photo of a fantastic memory, wrap up a bulb for their garden in spring, or source the perfect cup for their tea. The cost of Christmas and our other calendar celebrations can be completely overwhelming and consistently lands enormous debts at the feet of families already struggling.

We need to remember that, ultimately, we are all really looking for connection, not stuff.

Gifts are just symbols, after all. Historically, gifts were exchanged at Christmas time as a way of showing love and affection. They were symbols, and this was understood. A gift would often be homemade, and it would be a small token to show the recipient that they were held in high regard, that they were loved, or that they were part of the community, part of the family. The sharing of provisions during the leaner winter months was generally a theme for Christmas gifting in the northern hemisphere and people would exchange these little symbolic gifts of sweets, cakes, preserves and dried fruits, as well as handicrafts such as little knitted socks and mittens, or embroidery on handkerchiefs;

just small things that you could have passed hand-to-hand, perhaps wrapped in paper with a little ribbon.

We have lost sight of presents as symbols of our love, and we feel the pressure to gift as if each gift was the sum total of all of our love, wrapped up; each year having to go further, to stretch to something bigger and more exciting. This has led to a culture and a climate where there is an expectation, a pressure, to stretch our budget and spend more than we can really afford in an attempt to prove how important someone is and to show them how much we love them.

What we give to the people we love at these points in the year is not all of our love; it's just a small, simple token of that love – a symbol.

The whole of our love plays out in our everyday actions and we can't wrap that up. It's beyond priceless. Come back to this reminder if you are ever struggling through lack of funds to treat your people to the things you think they deserve – your true gift is given all year. It's impossible to wrap. It's your time and your effort. I also urge you not to fall into the trap of overcompensation for lack of time and energy throughout the year, with big flashy gifts on birthdays and holidays. It never works, and you're far better off gifting a small token along with a note sharing your love and commitment to the relationship. That will be remembered and treasured way longer than any huge box you can drag back from a shop.

One issue that seems to crop up a lot for those who are trying to embrace the Not Needing New mindset, is the question of what to do when you don't want to keep a gift that has been given to you? There are times when you will be given a present by someone you love, but you don't want to keep the gift and you fear being discovered if you try to pass it on. It can be really tricky and can cause real emotional hurt to those we love if we later seem to 'reject' an item that we were bestowed.

Likewise, it can also be considered too blunt, too rude, too ungrateful to request not to be a recipient. Some people love to give and in being told 'no thank you', they may feel that they are denied an important part of what they need in the relationship.

I truly believe that there are nuances here and if you can employ them in the right way for the right people, all will be well.

Sometimes you know that the person giving the gift needs to be loved and appreciated more than you need to have your freedom from clutter. Take, for example, my stepdad's mother, Irene, giving me a mustard yellow pair of thick nylon tights for Christmas when I was fifteen or sixteen. The colour was either fifteen years too late, or twenty-five years too early, to be cool. I was so mortified to see this weird hosiery item, having unwrapped the little parcel, that I really struggled not to laugh out loud, especially as my older sister (equally horrified) was saying, 'Oh lucky Anna! They're nice.'

Irene, a widow, had come into our lives by virtue of her only child, her son, marrying our mum, a recently divorced woman with nine children. We were a massive tribe of kids in the midst of a horrible family breakdown and rearrangement. Irene went from having to give one present at Christmas, to trying to find the right things for her new 'family' of eleven. She knitted animals for the younger ones, but as a teen, I was given a gift that she probably felt was rather fun and edgy for a teenage girl. The trouble was, she had been a teenage girl during the Second World War when life was pretty different. I hated the tights, but I understood the thought and I loved that I had been included. Irene lived miles away and only saw us a couple of times a year, so it was easy to get away with never having to wear the mustard tights and not having to fear giving them away to anyone who might bump into her.

In this situation I still think that the best thing to do was to not lie about how much I loved them and would wear them, but give authentic thanks for remembering me and for being kind. And then later, passing them on to another person who would make good use of them. No feelings harmed, no damage done, no lies told.

Be careful of the pitfalls of 're-gifting'. If you are going to pass on a gift from a friend that you know you will not use, do not hand it into the PTA raffle of the school that you're both parents at, or give it to the nearest charity shop. Be a bit more discreet and make sure that it travels further afield.

In other situations, I think you can benefit from being open and transparent from the outset. Letting your family know what would be useful in the run-up to a gifting period is a great idea and people are generally very grateful to be given some idea of what to give you that will be truly wanted and used. Alternatively, asking your friendship group if everyone is happy to skip a year of gifting can be a truly relieving moment for all of you. Agreeing to meet up to do something fun in the new year instead is often appreciated by everyone, who may well have been feeling the burden of even more stuff, for the sake of stuff, needing to be bought and wrapped.

I know a family who once wrapped all their little gifts to each other in terry-towelling nappies and pinned them shut with nappy pins so that all the 'wrapping' could be given to the parents of the new baby expected in the new year.

In my massive family, we now have an annual Sibling Secret Santa with a strict 'no more than, no less than' budget, with its own message group and another place where you can write to your anonymous Santa and drop them an idea of what will be most appreciated if you don't want to leave it to chance. Telling people what you want isn't ruining the festival, it's reducing waste and helping them avoid the awful sense that they have to trawl the shops to 'just get anything'.

Decorations

When it comes to decorations and the lure of turning our homes into supremely tasteful seasonal masterpieces, I think it's time we took a pause to consider who these decorations are for. Rather than feeling that you have to select a new theme every year and colour-coordinate the whole set-up for the perfect photo, it's far more rewarding to focus on building strong traditions that meet the need we all have for familiarity, community and excitement. I treasure my box of birthday and holiday decorations that comes out year after year, lovingly added to over time, with newer memories nestling in with those from the distant past. It has become a really important part of our celebration to unwrap the baubles and untangling the bunting, with all the memories flowing out with them. Every single one holds significance in my little family unit and seeing our shared history bringing colour and joy to the home is everything. The warmth you will feel from keeping and treasuring your cache of long-loved decorations is so wonderful and could never be replaced by a yearly update that moves on to a charity shop or a bin as soon as the last mince pie has been eaten. Even the hilariously bad nursery offerings made with painted pasta and cotton wool have a charm that makes us smile every time they get pulled back out.

Outfits

Outfits are another area where I believe we could all step back from the pressure to present perfectly and resist the consumer madness. There is an almost accepted notion among many that we will all have a brand-new outfit on for every occasion. Look around at all the shops and the supermarkets and the environmentally disastrous sequins everywhere in the run-up to the big seasonal events. It's a lovely thing to dress up for a celebration and I agree that these annual dinners are truly special occasions, but I encourage you to think about whether you already own anything that you could wear to look and feel special. The chances are that you already have something really fabulous that you could whip out and no one would feel disappointed in you! Get your accessories on, go to town with what you already own and you're ready to welcome in anything new you may be gifted, without having to feel guilty about the new outfit you felt you had to buy for one meal with your own family and friends. I promise you,

you'll start to feel a new and wonderful happiness creeping in when you are proud of yourself for having an equally good time at your special occasions using the things that you already had.

Now we have covered gifting, decorations and outfits, here are some ideas of how to enjoy these special days without overspending or buying too much stuff that people may not really want:

- Making tokens for actions – doing things for people is a brilliant way to show your love. Anything from babysitting, to baking a cake, to painting a wall, or mowing the lawn – a little handmade voucher that your friend can call into use when it suits, is a lovely gift to make and give to someone special.

- Making things in advance for the celebration, like creating a garland from gathered greenery, or baking little treats and bagging them up in a beautiful way – these small things can be done as a family and will become part of a tradition which will be so significant for the family in years to come. The time spent on these small actions will become the memories forever associated with the festival and will begin to hold more magic than the gifts, just as you remembered the customs that felt important for you in the task earlier.

- Joining up with friends or family and having a shared event, perhaps hiring a bigger space to do so (youth hostels rent out whole premises to groups over holiday breaks). This democratises big events and creates an atmosphere of collaboration and community. You'll find that you can afford to make use of some really great places if you share the cost between a few families.

- Share the catering. Asking others to bring one element creates a sense that the whole group were able to support each other; it really cements the idea of community and takes the burden of cost and work away from one individual who may feel overwhelmed. Remember that over-catering can be a real problem in terms of food waste, so having one person who can coordinate the offerings is really useful, and make sure that there are ways to divvy up and redistribute leftover food using suitable containers.

- Have a family secret gift exchange with a budget limit. Having a charity-shop challenge is an incredibly enjoyable and sustainable way of managing gifting when there are many people. Children can be included, or not if the family prefer to gift newer things to the kids, but they often really enjoy having a small budget and looking though charity shops to choose a special gift for someone by themselves.

- Have a drawer space throughout the year where you squirrel away bits and pieces when you see them in charity shops or in sales, ready to give to others. Spreading the gathering time across the whole year will enable you to save so much money, as you will steadily build up a collection of the 'right' things for people, negating the need to panic-buy later on.

- One specifically Christmas idea I read and loved was the idea of forgoing the cheap plastic cracker gifts, instead passing around an old biscuit tin filled with a selection of all the bits that usually live in that 'bits drawer' we all have in our homes somewhere! The safety pins, small screwdrivers, rulers, batteries, cotton reels – everyone gets to pick a thing that will be useful for them.

- Finally, how about disappearing altogether? Having a short break away and not even getting involved in present giving and huge meals, simply opting out and enjoying your own rhythm for a couple of days can be the perfect way to handle the holiday hysteria for some.

Task: Your Hopes for Celebrations

In order to start working out what you are hoping for during your big celebrations of the year, let's focus on one and try to break it down. Can you think of the three most important words to describe what you are looking for from the celebration? For example, family time/relaxation/laughter – (write them into spaces) then follow the arrows – consider one action you can take to get this to happen (maybe watching a film together, maybe cooking a meal together). Can it be bought? What will facilitate it? Do you already have the tools to make this happen?

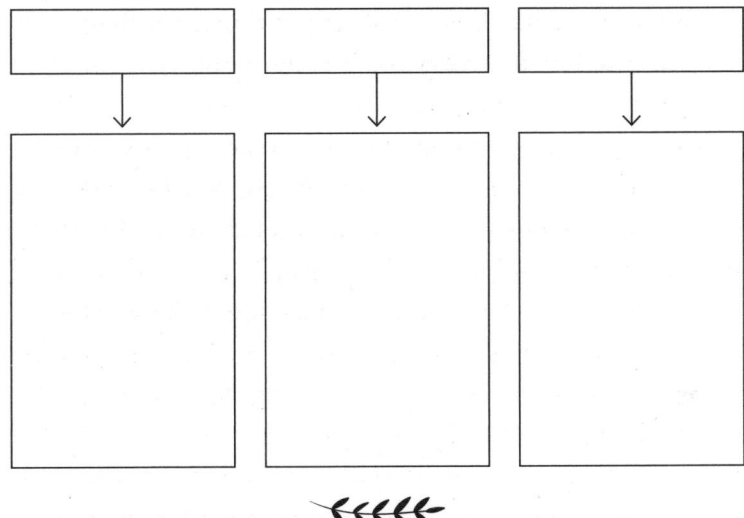

GOING AWAY ON HOLIDAY

Now for the other sort of holiday – the going away kind. Does adopting a Not Needing New lifestyle impact holidays? The short answer is no. Not Needing New is all about being content with less physical stuff and being able to feel happy with a dialled-back experience of consumerism. Travel isn't necessarily 'stuff', it's an experience, and valuing experiences over the accumulation of objects is a fundamental part of enjoying a life with fewer things. Hopefully, a Not Needing New approach to having a holiday will help you to see that holidays don't have to come with eye-watering costs or a shopping list of essentials every time you head off somewhere.

What we want from a vacation-type holiday is very similar to the celebration times; we want a change, a break from the norm, a chance to do less, or do more, an opportunity to feel that life is offering us something else. We want to see new things, to seek connection, perhaps with our partners, our children, our friends, or perhaps with ourselves if we are travelling solo. We look for 'good' weather, whether that be sunshine or snow, we want good food, possibly more alcohol than usual and experiences that we can remember for ever. Sometimes the most memorable and binding experiences are not the picture-perfect scenes of travel brochures.

I started this book by describing my first holiday with my then-new partner, in a tent, in Wales. Let me now tell you about our first foreign holiday together in the hope that you will find some common ground in my experience of recognising the value of 'Type 2 Fun'.

As we approached the long winter back in 2015, I had an offer to escape to a friend's apartment in Lanzarote and we all became highly excited about it for various reasons. For my young son, it was the knowledge that there was a really good petrol go-karting track on the island and kids could drive the cars. For my small daughter, it was the idea of staying right next to a turquoise pool. For me it was the joy of jetting off to a place where, for a short while, we could feel the warmth of the sun on our pale faces and not constantly fear the cost of heating our home. It was an interesting holiday, going together with a fairly new partner and his three young girls, and I learnt a lot about shared holidays on a budget.

We experienced, in no particular order: an airline fine for an extra bag, an 'incident at security' involving the floor manager and the five glue sticks / a collection of brass antique bullets that my children had packed in their hand luggage, a race for the departure gate which included a child's shoelace trapped in a travelator and some screaming; at the apartment, five beds for seven people, an accident on a remote deserted beach involving a tooth fully puncturing through a face, the upholstery of the only seven-seater car available to hire on the island suffering the fate of a car-sick child, and the agony of a small boy almost constantly asking to go go-karting!

This initiation into family holidays has gone down in our collective memory because it was filled with so many things we hope we won't have to face ever again on a trip away. In a time when we were seeking relaxation, ease, connection and comfort, we ended up with a maelstrom of mini-mishaps that made the whole holiday feel exhausting. In the fullness of time, however, we had a good laugh about it and developed a real sense of bonding over this shared experience. We pinned some core memories as a group; one of my boyfriend's kids told me that it's a known thing, and that we can refer to this holiday as 'Type 2 Fun': not always fun in the moment, but fun to look back on.

Now, I'm not suggesting that you should aim for stressful or unpredictable holidays; I simply tell this story as a reminder to you, and to me, that even the best-laid plans for a fabulous holiday can go awry. We pin so much hope and expectation on our short breaks away and forget that the real memories come from the people you experience the holiday with and the opportunity to see something new.

Memory building is a very important part of the psychology of holidays; when life keeps ticking along in its usual smooth pattern, it can be impossible to review past months or years and to pick out any feelings associated with the times. We need to have peaks, and the occasional trough, to attach our recollections to and anchor them in our life story. 'Type 2 Fun' is therefore valid, even if it's not the type that we enjoy at the time. It can be a hugely important part of human connection.

The fact that holidays serve to pin down important family memories means that this can be achieved whatever the cost, whatever the budget is that we have. There is no requirement to spend thousands on a luxurious break in order for the time to embed itself deeply within our memories and to create a shared experience that will be treasured for decades.

All of the different motivators that we look to fulfil when booking holidays, be it adventure, rest, connection, isolation, action, relaxation, cultural immersion, language-learning, romance, whatever the driving emotions are, can be found in a myriad of ways and with vastly differing budgets.

I can assure you that having had the extraordinary luck in life to have both dined and spent a night at Raymond Blanc's legendary Le Manoir aux Quat'Saisons Hotel, and to have wild-camped in the back of a Ford Transit secretly parked up by the white sand of a tiny remote Welsh bay, that the latter (despite the inferior toilet arrangements) felt profoundly life-affirming in a way that no luxury hotel ever could.

The key point to this chapter is to remind you that taking holidays is important and not something that you need to deny yourself in the quest for minimalism or contentment with less. We all need to break up the monotony of the daily grind. Humans have been enjoying holidays and celebrations of all kinds for as long as we can track. We do not have to forgo allowing ourselves these times, but we can consider how our choices of where to go and how will have an impact. Transport and accommodation impact our environment and communities in terms of emissions and the scarcity of affordable housing for locals; we can be more mindful of this. We can definitely reduce our impact on our own economic resources, and global resources, by realising that we don't need a suitcase full of new outfits and travel products to visit a new place. The clothes that you already have and love will still be wonderful in a new place; remember that when you are away from home, no one has seen your 'old' outfits either, so no one will even know if you have a whole new collection or if you're wearing everything you've had for ever.

Here are a few alternative ways to holiday:

- House swaps – You can do this with family and friends but there are also some great websites and associations where you can sign up and connect with people who are interested in swapping houses for a break. I did this once and had a week in a stunning farmhouse overlooking the Menai Straits in Anglesey, while the family who lived there were at my rather less inspiring home, in order that they could have an easy and inexpensive place to stay with their teenage triplet sons while visiting elderly relatives in the south-east of England. It worked extremely well for both families and we were able to explore an area we had never been to on a really small budget, from the vantage point of someone in the community. → https://www.homeexchange.com/

- Pet-sitting – Again, there are established companies who will team up people looking to go away and leave their beloved pets at home with a sitter, with others who are happy to care for the animals while enjoying time away in a new place. I know people who are currently living their entire lives going from one of these pet-sitting posts to another, exploring the globe. ➜ https://www.trustedhousesitters.com

- Mini-breaks – Nothing ground-breaking here, but just a reminder that even three nights away can feel like a decent sojourn. There is a fabulous British television programme called *Travel Man* that I come back to time and again to seek inspiration for European short breaks and to see how possible it is to pack a huge number of experiences into forty-eight or seventy-two hours with a limited budget. There are ways to keep the cost right down. I recommend choosing the least popular hours to travel, taking all your own food for the journeys, stick to the baggage limit and just see how long you can go on a couple of pairs of knickers and a toothbrush! If you can, repurpose a set of tiny bottles to use for your toiletries (I once took toothpaste in an old Vaseline lip balm tin), and final tip, I have discovered, via my boyfriend, that the average supermarket Bag for Life is the exact dimensions allowed as a cabin bag on a budget airline. ➜ https://www.channel4.com/programmes/travel-man-48-hours-in

- Staycations – This involves imagining that you are a tourist in your own locale; trying to see it with fresh eyes. What have you not explored? This kind of break potentially eliminates the cost of accommodation and reduces the travel costs to a bare minimum, freeing up funds to try activities that would otherwise be off-limits. For us, this would include doing organised high-ropes courses, visiting trampoline parks, going to a safari park and eating out in a café or restaurant. These daytrips lumped together into a holiday at home can be the source of many precious memories. If your version of a staycation means staying somewhere a little fancier within your local area then go for it! You're still saving on travel and you're still having a holiday from domestic pressures.

- Van life – I'm throwing this in as someone who has had some amazing trips away in the back of a builder's van, swept out and furnished with a mattress and some fairy lights. Do you have a van in your life? If so, make a van trip happen!

- Wwoofing – The acronym 'WWOOF' originally stood for Working Weekends On Organic Farms. Now it's sometimes referred to as 'Willing Workers On Organic Farms' or 'World Wide Opportunities on Organic Farms'; there are many autonomous national groups under this umbrella where you can exchange your energy and willingness to pitch in and work, hands-on and learning, in sustainable agriculture for the chance to have bed, board and bonhomie with other lovely folk. → https://wwoof.org.uk

- Road trip of visits to friends/family – Staying with family and friends for a night is amazing. Staying for longer can run the risk of becoming difficult, no matter how much you all love each other and how many years you go back. It can work really well to plan a little road trip where your route drops by on a few different welcoming homes in succession, where you can stash up on a boot full of lovely food items to bring and share while you spend a night under the roofs of your dearest people.

- Camping – Since the rise in popularity of glamping, it's no longer the preserve of those who would have a summer break under a fly-sheet, crossing their fingers and cooking flaccid bacon in the rain; there are now camping options for everyone almost all year round, even in our very unpredictable UK climate. As a massive family group, this is our way of being able to afford to get together, as none of us has a home big enough for this many siblings and their family members. We have an annual trip to the awesome campsite at Eweleaze Farm in Dorset, where 'Camp Kilpatrick' often extends to more than thirty-five people – can you imagine the hotel bill we would run up trying to all stay in the same place for a few days? Campsites are a fabulous option for large group adventures where the focus is all about the connection rather than the opulence.

HIGH DAYS AND HOLIDAYS

Task: The Anti-Holiday

When we were young, we used to love to play the 'anti-gift' game and the 'anti-holiday' game – making ourselves fall about laughing by imagining the least appropriate present or holiday for a particular person. Just for fun, can you imagine what your anti-holiday would be like? What, to you, would be the least desirable type of holiday break from all the popular options? Is it a cruise (I think mine is)? Skiing? Backpacking? An all-inclusive poolside? What is it that you really dislike the thought of? Can you use the things that you back away from to identify the things that you are seeking?

_____

_____

_____

_____

_____

_____

_____

_____

_____

When you work out a few things that you do want from a holiday, can you see any opportunities to bring these feelings into your ordinary life in a spend-free way? For example, if you're looking to 'switch off' or if you identify a deep desire to disconnect from work pressure and family responsibilities, can you regularly book in one Sunday afternoon a month to walk alone / get a massage / have a phone-free day? This much smaller intervention to give yourself what you need will help to keep you feeling content and less likely to feel suffocated by the many stresses of our lives.

When you do know where you're heading and it's time to get packing, travelling as light as possible is always such a great goal to have. Even if you're not flying, managing to restrict yourself to a minimum weight of baggage to haul around with you is so liberating and can also give you the opportunity to bring one or two really worthwhile things home (for me, it's always soap). If I'm flying, knowing that the size of a small cabin bag is almost exactly the same size as a supermarket bag for life, I have been known to simply use one of these to go away for a long weekend, no fancy luggage needed.

I try to stick to the 5,4,3,2,1 rule with the bag: five days of undies, four tops, three bottoms, two pairs of shoes (wear one when travelling), one jacket or coat. I keep any tiny bottles that come my way throughout the year for decanting a little bit of shampoo into, and one for bringing enough clothes washing liquid to launder a few things in the bathroom basin so that I can keep rotating the clothes I have chosen. I often pop in a pouch of savoury rice or a bag of pasta so that even if I turn up at late o'clock and have no open shop nearby, I can make something to get through the first disorienting night without spending loads on emergency eating at late-night restaurants.

Keeping this way of packing in mind also stops me from feeling tempted by all the alluring summer collections that start dropping in the shops from the beginning of May. I won't have room (or need) for multiple beach cover-ups or sandals and bikinis in every colour, so there is absolutely no need to buy them.

An easy way to save money when travelling, without missing out on having the experiences of dining in lovely places, is to plan your day around eating out for breakfast rather than going to the restaurants in the evenings. Menu choices can be wonderfully fresh and varied in the morning, and eating out as the sun comes up with the whole day stretching ahead is a lovely thing to do. It generally costs significantly less than a meal in the same location in the evening and usually you won't be drinking so much alcohol!

And one more top tip, always check out the local transport options from the airport into the town or city that you are heading for. Private transfers are often proffered by travel companies at the point of booking, but hopping onto the local bus or train will be a sliver of the cost, you will see more of the destination and its character, and you will be with the local residents who live and work around the travel hubs so you'll always have knowledgeable people near who can point you in the right direction.

Enjoy your holidays – those at home and those in far-off places. You do not have to reduce your appetite for fun and adventure if you're aiming for a life with less clutter. As the postcard often reads, 'I'd rather have a passport full of stamps than a house full of stuff.'

CHAPTER 9

Creating a Home

In the seven years that followed the day that our lives changed, I moved house with my small children seven times.

It's true what is said about moving – that after divorce it's the most stressful thing that happens to adults (I'm not putting bereavement into this ranking because it's too far off the scale). In that time I went from the four-bedroom house to a flat for three days (until the house sale fell through at the eleventh hour), back to the empty house, then to a school boarding house, which almost finished me off, followed by an unplanned escape to my new partner's two-bedroom house where seven of us squeezed in for eighteen months, before a ridiculously overpriced ordinary rented house I wasn't able to manage for a year, back to the partner's house while I recovered and searched, and then, finally, the safety of my own tiny flat.

Each of these moves was a wrench. Each time everything we possessed had to be packed into boxes and moved, never by a professional firm, just by ourselves, in a Transit van. The children had their belongings whipped away and stored, unboxed and spread out, packed back up again and hidden away in plastic tubs, so often, that we just eventually lost track of what was where and which things were wanted, which were outgrown, what was needed, and what we still had.

Every time we found ourselves in a new place, I held hope that it was going to be our proper base for a while and that the children would be able to settle and feel a sense of belonging. I wanted a sense of belonging. I had no other family in the county to be the steady foundations and I craved a base that felt solid and permanent enough to harbour two small children whose little lives had been flipped upside down by the family heartbreak of the stroke and of the collapse of the unit that we had been part of.

When you are creating your home, there is absolutely nothing as important as the safety and comfort of your own familiar things and the autonomy you have within the walls of that building. It doesn't matter one jot if you have the latest, most fashionable interior trends, the biggest spaces, or the funkiest building, if you have no true sense of connection to the fabric within, and if you have a feeling that it's someone else's space, you will struggle to truly be living in your home.

I say this because it's a comfort to those of us who fall foul of the creeping doubt that we've done 'well enough' if we live in small places without the appliances, rooms, furniture and larger spaces of our friends and family. I want you to hear that the single most important way that you can create a wonderful home with less, is to be in a place that feels safe for you and your group, and to be in possession of the basic things that you need to function, and to connect you to a feeling of comfort. You do not need to be featured in a glossy interiors magazine to be the creator of a marvellous and beautiful home.

There are some key aspects of getting by with less that I will share with you here. Some are tips and ideas for a low-spend, more sustainable way of decorating, and some are simply thoughts on the mindset of home and what is important for the people within.

Forget the Postcode

Despite the title of the long running British television series, *Location, Location, Location,* the truth is that it doesn't matter where your home is. It isn't the placement, the style, the materials, the size – it's the sense of home within that makes it a home. How you achieve that is down to your own group culture, and how you do that is by setting traditions and forming a cultural fabric for yourself and those who live with you. It's the way that you live; the routines and the tools that surround you. We all hold memories of the homes we have visited throughout our lives, thresholds that we have stepped over and feelings that we have picked up from being included in those homes. There will be places that felt instantly warm and welcoming, places that you delighted in, homes where you wanted to stay longer and wanted to take a piece of inspiration back home to your own life. There will also be homes where you felt less at ease and where you didn't feel relaxed and able to slot into the atmosphere. If you think about these diametrically oppositional experiences of being in other homes, it's quite likely that it wasn't about the type of sofa, the colour of the paint, the style of the banisters, their choice of flooring, or the postcode; it was far more likely to do with the human behaviour of the people within and how that was affecting you. It's so much more than the stuff. We need to understand that.

The most wonderful homes can be found anywhere. That is our start.

Forget the Size

Having said that you don't need to be featured in the pages of a glossy magazine for your home to be wonderful, would you believe I was once written about and photographed in my tiny flat, looking all tidy and pulled together, by a most well-respected journalist, Hugh Stevens. Hugh is a former award-winner of the International Property Journalist of the Year Award, the Lifestyle and Interiors Journalist of the Year, and the UK Property Journalist of the Year, and writes regularly for *The Times* in their property magazine, *Bricks and Mortar*. He contacted me via Instagram, having seen some of the posts that I had shared, as he was writing a feature on tiny living and the cosy appeal of sleeping nooks. It felt extraordinary to be considered worthy of being written about by such a leading journalist in such a well-considered publication, and I was delighted that my very small flat, furnished almost exclusively from thrifted stuff found at the council tip, plundered from skips and found in charity shops, was going to be celebrated in a mainstream broadsheet read by so many.

With all the perfect familiarity of things not turning out quite as wonderfully as they could, the single biggest national news item for seventy years broke on the eve of printing and the entire magazine print was pulled. There was nothing anyone could do, not even Hugh.

The Queen died.

Despite all the emotions in the wake of such a shock, it was still an incredible experience to realise that the combination of 'second-hand' and 'small' was capable of making it into such a publication. There was room being made, by the writers in charge of discussing home styling, for homes that had been put together on shoestring budgets and with real limitations of space.

This felt like such an encouraging moment for me and, hopefully, for so many other people who were without vast incomes and houses. The way that I had made it into Hugh's intended piece was by showing that with some imagination and careful editing of what I could get hold of, I had managed to put together a really interesting living space with a miniscule spend and a massive lean into re-using old things.

The key to getting this 'right' is that it needs to be right for you. That's all. There are, and there have been, so many property programmes on our screens where the focus has been on decorating for growth, on maximising the highest profits from the subsequent buyer, that I think it has left us all feeling that our time in a home is less valid than the potential preferences of hitherto imagined persons who might be interested in the place in a decade. I appreciate that for the private rental households, roughly 20 per cent of the UK, things are very different, and there are very few changes that can be made, but my experience with the flat was all based on the fact that as a full-time Head of English in a school, having taught for over twenty years, I was incredibly lucky to find a mortgage provider that would lend me just enough to secure this two-bedroom, no garden, no balcony, no central heating flat, as a single person and so I was saved from the ridiculous trap of paying almost double what my own mortgage is now, in rental payments to someone else to cover their mortgage (and more) on their second property.

Regardless of whether you own or rent your current place, the way that you decide to put your stamp on it is going to be what makes it the most perfect home for you, and as your home is essentially an inward-facing reflection of your style, you do not have to think about the outward show it's putting on for anyone else. Contrary to the inescapable truth of clothes forming the interface at which we meet the outside world, so therefore bringing a degree of inescapable judgement, the inside of your home has no obligation to meet anyone or invite any exposure that you do not wish to control. Very importantly, creating a home is far more than the aesthetic and the objects that you put in; it's actually the emotion; the feeling of safety, comfort and familiarity that will create a homely atmosphere for you and your family. If you're browsing websites, trying to select a hotel room, or an Airbnb space, and you're considering what would be a really good choice for a short stay, it's quite likely that you will be drawn to clean, minimal, light-filled and uncluttered rooms rather than cosy nooks with pictures, ornaments, fridge stickers, games, washing hanging up to dry, and personal touches that tell human stories. One is not better than the other, but one is definitely more 'homelike' and when we are able to identify that, we understand what sorts of visual clues tell us that a room is actually a home.

It's been great to see articles, blogs and Pinterest boards about how to live well in small spaces, that there's a growing trend for media coverage on 'tiny house living' as rents and mortgages have become harder for us to manage.

These insights often describe the most beloved tools – a special candle-holder, a book shelf, a coffee pot, a dog bed – which support the highly personal routines that the home-maker has made space for in their limited environment, helping the reader to understand that each carefully considered inclusion was evaluated less for its aesthetic or the adherence to trend than for the joy that it brings just by existing. In this way, the curation of stuff is simplified down through the leanest of filters: if it isn't useful, it's not included, and if it is useful then let it also be beautiful.

Forget the Trends

When we have a little more space to play with, we tend to quickly fill it. But what does your home say about you? A primetime television gameshow in the eighties called *Through the Keyhole* invited a trio of celebrity panellists to ascertain the identity of another mystery celebrity by watching footage of an outside broadcast presenter wandering around a house and providing a series of clues and red herrings about to whom it may belong. It was such fun to try to work out who the mystery celebrity was from the clues that lay in plain sight all around their homes.

This is a lovely starting point to consider what, for you, are the clues that would tell others that your home is yours. How does your safe space reflect your values?

Through this keyhole, can you pick out a few items from your home that can tell the story of you?

NOT NEEDING NEW

Task: Through the Keyhole

You are the mystery celebrity. What indirect clues are in the objects of your home that would identify you? Which objects tell your story? Write them in the keyhole below.

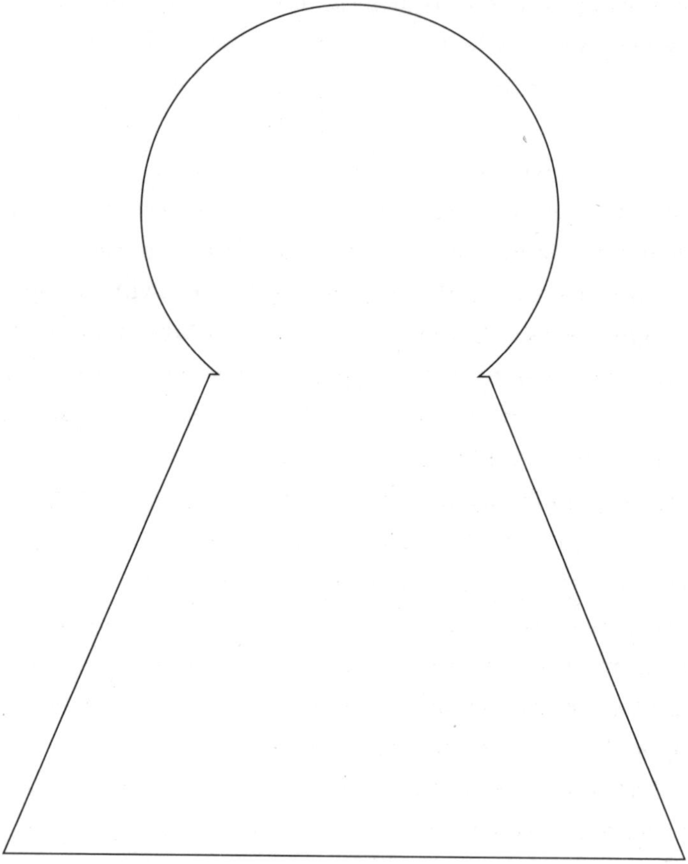

These are the things that make your home truly yours. The things that an impersonal Airbnb, even a stunningly gorgeous one, would never be able to replicate.

These tokens and clues about you, the souvenirs from travelling along in your life, are essentially a little museum of you and of your family. They are the most important elements to nest-building. This is why, if you're constantly upgrading and redecorating, continually redesigning and dressing your space with only the fashionable decor touted in mags, you're missing out on creating an important attachment with your possessions – one, which I would argue, will give you a deep sense of security and grounding. We can all appreciate a lovely hotel with minimalistic design, clean lines, and the latest neutral decor, chosen to offer a sense of space without feeling like the awkward guests in someone else's home, but something in our innate human nature does call to us to feather our nests with those things that trigger memories of being loved, being safe and being happy. They could be anything: photographs, pebbles from a certain beach, the jug that your grandma used. Little things are really important when building a home, so I would suggest that it can be a mistake to stash your non-fashionable treasures away in boxes in the loft. Try to keep some meaningful items close to you and in everyday usage, for sadly, as we all know, saving everything for best, or for another vague day, can be a mistake that we realise too late.

Creating a welcoming home can be as simple as having teabags in, even if you don't drink tea – being ready to offer a visitor some physical symbol that serves to tell them that they can sit and stay for a while and enjoy your company. I encourage you to actually tell people that they are welcome too. We often feel it, and think it, but we forget to explicitly say to the people we like being around, 'You're welcome to pop over / I'd love you to come over.' I have an ex-colleague who is so good at this; she often writes social media messages to her friends and reminds us that there will always be a welcome at her home, there will always be a drink and a seat and chat to be shared. I don't live very near and I haven't dropped by, but my heart knows that I would be welcomed in and I know that her home would be a beautiful place of warmth and joy, no matter the age or colour of the sofa – what better projection of a home could we want?

The most wonderful homes are created by the emotional responses we engage with when we spend time within. This is great news and, indeed, I have been so encouraged and grateful for the attitudes of my children's friends to our tiny flat. Far from being embarrassed by having such a limited space to live in, my children have shared how their friends love this little flat filled with thrifted things and they actually want to come over to be here.

When it comes to creating a space perfectly suited to you and one that you know will envelop your visitors in the authentic warm experience of being welcomed into your world, the one thing you really need to build is – you guessed it – confidence. Just as with Chapter 6 earlier, Fashion v. Style, you have to allow yourself the freedom to like the things that you like. (Remember the list you made in Chapter 3 – what *you* liked without being influenced by anyone else.)

When you instantly love something, be it a spoon, a candlestick, a mirror, a chair, you need to focus on your gut reaction over any doubts about its contemporary fashion aesthetic. It's really easy and, if I'm honest, sometimes really exciting, to go to large stores like TK Maxx, IKEA, Zara Home, etc. and pick up a load of beautiful, bang-on-trend little accent pieces to dress your home and to freshen up the style. You'll be rewarded with an interior that will be judged to be pleasing and contemporary by the majority of people who get to see it, but you won't be able to capture that richness of self, that tapestry of truth that comes from building your style from the singular elements that you have collected and curated over time.

When I began shopping second-hand for my home, if I spotted something quirky in a charity shop or down at the tip, I would immediately be drawn to it. I would pick it up and think about whether I could make that thing work for me in my home. Sadly, so many times the initial wave of connection that made me pick it out would be drowned out by the voice that told me it was ugly, it was embarrassing, it was old, it was weird, and so I left things behind, not because they had no use, or I had no emotional response to them, but because I didn't trust myself to like something without the approval and validation of someone else.

Over time, there were occasions when I went away, went back home, and couldn't stop thinking about the thing I had walked away from. This is never a feeling I get from items in big chain stores. Sometimes there's a calling and I advise you to listen to yourself. As with that list in Chapter 3, something that you are drawn to and are unable to stop thinking about is a thing that will stand the test of time in your home and is worth your care and attention.

So despite the solid advice to 'WAIT, Visualise' when

at the point of buying any ubiquitous stuff from the huge chains, my tip for creating your own stylish space is simply do not ignore the instant emotional reactions that you will have for certain, rare items. What is fashionable will constantly change and need updating. Your treasure radar is alert to your own style, it's beyond fashion, and it will work for you. Remember that fashion and style are not the same thing – be it clothes or interiors. Your gut instinct can be relied upon to help you create the most wonderfully stylish home from the loved things that you already own and from a whole world of second-hand options. The key is learning to trust your own taste and choices.

DECORATING AND STYLING

Where I have enjoyed the most success in decorating the flat, is where I've found a way to make the modest space work for my specific situation, not being limited by what I think 'should', or 'ought' to be included, or omitted. The fun things in here are the details that came from thinking outside the box, about what we three actually needed in our daily lives, and where we could put those things we needed. Three people who each wanted privacy, but only two bedrooms, led to the creation of the platform nook where my shelf-bed sits. One living space and no room for a table led to the table being sawn in half and attached to the kitchen counter as a breakfast bar instead.

The reason we often make mistakes in our home design is due to the fact that we sometimes feel there's a blueprint for a home that we need to stick to, even if it doesn't suit our way of living. We have a tendency to both hang on to a traditional idea that certain things must go in certain places, and to hold back from making changes to our spaces in case the next person to live there wouldn't like them. Make your home right for you.

You can do this by firstly considering what is not working for you. Perhaps you have a dining room with a table that no one uses, maybe that table just becomes the dumping ground for all the stuff that no one has carried upstairs, the clothes rack, and all the paperwork that no one wants to face. It might be that once a year it gets cleared for a special dinner, and that is all. In this case, I would seriously suggest letting go of the dining room. You're not using it; it's not an effective use of your space, the Queen isn't coming over anymore. Imagine your life without it there – is it really going to be any different?

Now, what would make a difference? Another bedroom? A place for yoga? A chill-out room? A gym? A playroom? Craftroom? There will be a use that serves you better than the big dining table that was never used. This is not only true of big spaces like that, even in a small flat like mine; there are choices to be made about whether to accommodate certain 'normal' things. I don't have a TV, for instance – there's nowhere to put a permanent screen without it dominating the space, so I just don't own one. I also don't have an ironing board because 99.9 per cent of the time, I don't bother to iron things and if I did, I would place a towel on the worktop and do it that way.

Right from the earliest days, we – particularly women and girls – are conditioned into aspiring for the 'perfect' home. We had toy homes and toy home accessories. We played with tissue-sized bedding in Barbie's Dream Home, we arranged tiny wardrobes and minuscule cutlery in the Sylvanian Family Country Mansion, we learnt how to set up a house by following the pictures on the boxes and mimicking all that we saw in all the homes we went to. Very rarely are we asked to think of new ways of using spaces to suit our lives, but that's the thing you'll need to do to make the most of your own home.

I loved coming to the realisation that many very wealthy people, with huge houses, have a room built especially to meet their basic human desire to be in a small, warm and safe-feeling space. The Snug. An instantly calming space, tiny snugs are deliberately built into grander homes so that the owners have a place to feel cosy and comfortable – an inherent human need. If you only have a tiny place, remember this – you already have your snug, you already have the exact thing that is trying to be replicated by wealthier people elsewhere.

When I worked as a housemistress in a boarding school shortly after my life fell to bits, I was conscious of the fact that the dorms and shared spaces needed to be softened, to feel more homely for the teenagers who would be living most of the week there. I tried to buck the trend a little bit and bring some sustainable values into the house by finding some of the furnishings from the community charity shop in the village where the boarding school was based; things like softer, homely curtains rather than institutional blinds. I sent each of the sixty-three girls a handwritten letter that summer inviting them to bring in a plant or cushion when they returned in September so that we could make the environment feel as normal and homely as possible. I painted a vine of flowers and leaves all the way down the handrail of the main entrance stairs and wanted to get an old record player and stacks of vinyl to put in the common room. These tiny touches were trying to be the sorts of things that humans look for when we're decorating a home and we want to establish a feeling of ownership.

Painting is probably the first thing that springs to mind when we imagine changing a space to make it right for us. It's an instant way to make everything feel fresh, to make use of the significant impact of colour upon our mood and our purpose for a room, and it's relatively cheap and easy to manage it ourselves. However, paint is notoriously difficult to get rid of without environmental damage to waterways and disposal systems, and nearly every single decorating project will include buying more paint than is used. Many local schemes are being set up to redistribute the 50 million litres of leftover paint that the UK manages to be responsible for each year, and these hubs are a great starting point to check what's available in your area before you head off to buy new materials. Obviously you may have your heart set on a particular colour, but for many people there will be areas that can be painted white and there will, no doubt, be hundreds of part-used tins of white being donated. Have a look at the fabulous website www.communityrepaint.org.uk where you can search for schemes in your locality and why it's important to try to use what we already have in circulation.

As we already know, style is completely personal and linked to external factors such as our geographical location and the materials used to build your space, as well as to the cultural influences that shape us. It's impossible to give a 'how to' style guide that will be the right fit for everyone, so my main advice is to trust yourself in loving what you love and to look beyond the norms if they are not calling you. I will give you a few pointers here if you're looking for ways to create your home using second-hand stuff; given time, it's entirely possible to find everything you will ever need in the rapidly expanding second-hand marketplace.

Top Tips for Second-Hand Home Styling:

- Look through boxes / racks of charity shop pictures to find good frames in which to place your artwork and photographs. Old vinyl record covers can make great pictures.

- Include industrial / institutional objects in the home (old shop fittings, retro school chairs, etc.); don't discount quirky items you occasionally find in charity shops for being too 'officey' – sometimes it can be very cool to include different objects like this.

- Look at the fabric sections of charity shops for inspiring materials to reupholster seat pads / cushions. Simple seat pads can be pushed out and covered using a staple gun.

- Old kitchen items like graters and hand whisks are often very well made and look interesting hanging on display rather than hiding in a drawer.

CREATING A HOME

- If something isn't 'trending' but you're drawn to it, listen to your calling. It will probably come back into fashion at some point and then you'll not be paying over the odds due to that one spotlight moment.

- Keep an eye on local Facebook marketplace groups for large items, like quality sofas, which can sell there for a tiny fraction of the original price when people move house.

- Furniture can be sanded, painted, waxed, the handles changed – look beyond the first glance to try to see potential in the overall shape and purpose of the piece.

- Enjoy your theme – coloured glassware, mid-century pottery, tapestry samplers; a small collection of useful things that you love can act as art as well as being functional.

- Seek natural materials – adding glass, pottery, wood, wool, etc. doesn't introduce extra chemicals / toxins into your home and items made from them tend to stand the test of time more robustly than modern plastic versions.

- Keep a wishlist so that you know what you need, and if it's a big thing (like a table), keep a note on your phone of the ideal measurements you're looking for. If you see something you fall in love with but do not need, allow yourself to decide on 'one in, one out' so that you can welcome it in knowing that you will pass something else on.

- The most important tip is to trust your gut. If something truly stands out for you, make space for it. Don't be led by someone else's taste. If you create your home with your own style, it will be perennial and you will not keep feeling the need to waste things by chasing a new aesthetic time and time again.

As I've mentioned before in this book, when you are able to hold onto good things and reuse them over and over again, you find that you build a relationship with them and you'll start to really treasure and respect these objects. This is contrary to all that consumer culture wants you to do, but it carries a feeling that no new shopping can give you. Having these emotional bonds with the well-used, inanimate objects that we share our homes with, creates experiences and memories in common with the other people who live there, and who grow up there.

You will find little shared stories are embedded into the most unlikely of things. I have one tile, rescued from the home I grew up in – an orange seventies bathroom tile – and if any of my siblings come to my flat and see it on the bathroom windowsill with the toothbrush jar sitting on top of it, they're instantly taken back to our funny old Oxford bathroom and a hundred stories of nit shampoo, pulling out the broken handle to 'lock' the door, or the time Sarah and I ate dozens of vitamin tablets as 'sweets' and were taken to the John Radcliffe Hospital.

CREATING A HOME

Task: The Cutlery Drawer

As a way to test the relationships with the objects in your house, have a think about the cutlery drawer. What's in there? What are your favourite pieces? Do you have a spoon that you avoid? Is there a 'best' fork? Which is your preferred teaspoon? Take a moment and write down what those items are.

_____

_____

_____

_____

_____

_____

_____

_____

If you live with other people, ask them about the cutlery – which items are their favourites and why? It's often really surprising to discover that more than one person in the same house will head for the one 'best' knife if they get the chance.

Does this teach you anything about the relationships that you / your family have with objects? And if so, perhaps it will help you to feel good about having fewer, better things in your future.

These object-to-human memories are often found in the most unlikely places, the uncelebrated little corners of the places we live our lives in. It's wonderful to keep records of these things that we recognise as home. So many of our family photographs are of the people we love in the exciting places we visit, but I absolutely cannot stress highly enough how magical it is, decades on, to see photos of the places that you lived your routine life in, too. It's rare that we do, but take time to record your rooms and spaces, to capture the ordinary, everyday of your home. The pictures on your walls, the washing basket, the jug on the windowsill – you'll be surprised in years to come just how beautiful it is to see these details.

CHAPTER 10

Parenting with Enough

If you don't have or don't want children, or are far past the hands-on parenting phase, feel free to skip this section. For those of you currently parenting young people, it can be one of the hardest parts of having to make do with less, or making the decision to live with less than most of the other people within your social sphere. While it's comparatively easy to make the decision for yourself, and to steel yourself for any potentially difficult conversations when others wonder why you're not 'keeping up', when the choices that you make affect your children's relationships, even those choices that you make with pride and determination, can sometimes leave you feeling like you're doing the wrong thing. Like you're letting your children down in some way.

Generally, children do not have the subtlety and understanding needed when it comes to realising that we all have different access to resources and this is not a fault or failure. It's also usually true that children do not like to appear different to other children in any group because there's safety in similarity; if you stand out in any way, you'll be noticed for it and this is rarely comfortable for kids. Pretty much all bullying can be traced back to any sort of discernible difference; any departure from a 'norm' can be hard to handle, and in trying to look and behave in coherence with the herd majority, children are naturally and unconsciously demonstrating a deep survival instinct. As we get older and more confident, we hopefully move beyond this and feel strong enough to display our real and true selves without feeling so vulnerable to ostracism or criticism. So, it can feel hard to ask your children to be part of a Not Needing New culture whereby they will not be wearing what the 'cool kids' are, where they will not have the big fancy birthday parties of the popular kids and where they will not have access to the latest gadgets and toys that turn heads and establish them as members of the 'safe squad', ticking the right boxes in the culture of the groups.

A really important part of this is realising that no matter how clear and easy it is for us as adults to see that the stuff they want, and probably do not need, is just the short-lived stuff of trends and fads, for the children in that group environment, be it a school or club, it will feel incredibly important to fit in and have access to some of the things that their peers have access to.

There are many reasons for not wanting your child to have all the things that they want, but we will look at the two biggies: not wanting to promote overconsumption, and not having the money to buy the things they ask for anyway.

From a financial perspective, I would suggest honesty is a good starting point – be open about where you are with money, without scaring them into thinking that their safety is under threat. If, as a child, you are repeatedly just given the line, 'We can't afford it,' you may start to feel very worried about what other things your family won't be able to afford. A child who has these fears around money may also be sensitive and bottle up some of those fears and inadvertently intensify them in order to 'protect' the feelings of the grown-ups. Be open about having to make careful choices with the 'extra money' that you have, and framing it in that way will help a child not to feel that there is a threat to food or housing. This helps them to feel that there is a safe foundation which is separate to the more fun choices you can make with additional income from time to time.

Again, honesty is always a good way to proceed and if you are open with your child from the earliest of days and you demonstrate an attitude of only taking what you need, of valuing resources, of caring for possessions, of mending things and sharing, then to some degree at least, they will find it natural to accept and enjoy the culture of the home.

Supporting a child by showing interest in the things that they like is also really important. It's tempting to occasionally dismiss and sometimes to even want to laugh at some of the things that they become fixated on, especially when they are so removed from your own childhood experiences and your own understanding (an Xbox or those massive plastic sippy cups), when in actual fact it's much better for your relationship to acknowledge what they like, to look at it with them without criticising, to offer something that you like about it, and then let them know that although you don't have the funds, or you don't think that it's the right choice to be buying it right now, you do see why it's important to them and you will remember that they really liked it when there's next an opportunity where you or someone wants to get a gift that they'll really love.

You can ask them, if they're old enough, to send you links of items they like. You can suggest that you can look together online, and see if there are any second-hand versions; you can show children how to search for the same type of thing that they love and find it listed on a preloved site and explain to them how that works.

I have often found that showing the children some respect for their interests and likes is a very beneficial move. They tend to stop pushing and pushing for something if they've had a chance to show you what they like about it, a chance to talk about it, to look into it together and to hear some positive feedback from you. It's really good for your relationship to acknowledge their interests even when they are contrary to your own. When you have these foundations, the child will often accept any negative feedback much more easily as they won't feel that you're simply refusing their hope and being unreasonable. They will be much more likely to hear your helpful critique if you start off by listening to them and trying to understand the reasons that they have for finding something so appealing.

Before we get into more of the specifics of nurturing a Not Needing New mindset with children, here are a few really crucial bits of advice on parenting more generally that I think will be helpful to share. Of course, I'm not perfect or claiming to be an expert, but as someone who grew up with ten younger siblings, as a former teacher to hundreds of children and as the mother of two older young people (twenty-one and eighteen years old), I have had a good few decades to consider all the many things that have been important in helping us all to grow into becoming contented and decent people in the world. It feels like this book is a golden opportunity to share a little of that in the hope that these ideas will support you and empower you alongside your Not Needing New journey.

Like so much of the rest of this book, the most fundamental way that you will feel able to have a healthy and happy time as a parent, and in turn offer your children the same, comes from your inner conviction that you're doing the right thing and that you have your values aligning with your actions. It doesn't matter who tries to criticise what your choices are, if you feel deeply sure that what you are doing is right for you and your family, then you will not feel compelled to defend yourself, to argue your case, or to be hurt by alternative opinions. I can try to give you as much specific advice as I can to cover all scenarios, but you need to reassure yourself that you already know the right things for your unit. You will have a gut feeling. Parenting comes with no handbook, but there are a billion different words of advice coming at us from all directions. It can feel incredibly tricky to wade through it all, keeping all parties happy, when you're thrown out of your natural course of action by the myriad of advice coming at you. With that in mind, feel free to take my advice with a pinch of your own brand of salt!

I am in the fortunate position of having had twenty-three years of spending each working day with hundreds of children and, as hard as teaching is, I really do mean it when I say fortunate. It was an honour and, often, an absolute delight to have crossed paths with so many young families. Many times, I drove into my parking spot at school to be greeted by beaming ten-year-olds, leaning (safely) out of a ground-floor window, waving at me. What a delightful way to be welcomed into work each day.

But I was aware that even these wonderful children, who were so good with other people, and my own children, who are so good with other people, are not always so 'good' to their own parents. There are frequently times when I have 'that' conversation with my friends and with the parents of the children that I worked with – you know the one, where you joke that you should swap kids because they're so much nicer for other people than they are for you at home. They don't argue for others, they don't snap at them, demand things and treat them like servants.

And that's the way it should be. They are safe with you and they can test out all their feelings in a place where no harm will come. They must have a place where they assert their needs and desires, their truths and hurts, where they share their internal voice externally and you are the best place for that – you will love them no matter what, and they know that; it's why they can relax into raw honesty and where you can control what their internal voice hears back.

As crucial as your understanding and support of them is, though, it's also beneficial to think about when to pull back from being their everything and from being their kickboard. I'm going to list a few things that have stood out for me as a parent and a former teacher – a few tiny tweaks to reaffirm your role as parent, not as servant.

I readily admit that I am no 'perfect' parent (whatever that might mean) and that I too have been, and still can be seen, doing a few of the things I'm about to mention – but here are some things that I wish that I had been more aware of from the very beginning:

Let Your Child Self-Regulate

Give the baby/toddler times when they are not being stimulated by your loving face waving toys, singing, beaming, counting, quacking, mooing, etc. Let them have moments when they are awake and not at the centre of everything. They won't mind. You can leave a baby in a safe place while you fold the washing, unblock the U-bend or write your novel. I rarely did this. I thought I had to be the 'best' mother ever and I must have irritated the bejeezus out of my first child. My mistaken idea that being a 'good' parent meant attending to every waking moment with a purposeful display of attention and educationally enriching experiences left him unable to be left alone for the longest of times. Very early on, I was called back from my first day away (a friend's wedding) by the grandparents babysitting my six-month-old because they were unable to manage the hysterical scene caused by my absence. I wish I'd been calmer in my constant quest for the most profound mother–baby relationship. For both of us.

As odd as it might sound, I really think that there are times when giving your child space is the best choice for you, and for them. It's healthy for every human to have some space, and some boundaries. As parents, we are frequently signposted to believe that a full commitment involving every scrap of our attention and focus is the required recipe for a happy and successful child. As humans, in general, we have become increasingly incapable of allowing ourselves to have any moments in the day when we are bored. Both of these behavioural trends are impacting the way that we react and therefore build relationships with our children.

Not Every Group Is Their Group

My maternity leave was entirely structured around church halls and draughty rooms where I was paying (either in hard cash or by having to listen to Bible stories) for my tiny baby to be stimulated by something else. Music Groups, Baby Singing, Baby Signing, Baby Drama, Baby Swimming – my goodness, what a universe of opportunity there is. But actually, even though I did it because I was desperately lonely without the work staffroom and I wanted to be with people, it was hard to talk to other parents when you were supposed to be singing 'Where has Teddy Timmy gone?' and holding a parachute with one arm. I'd have been better off spending the £4 getting the bus to town with a mate and chatting, walking around a gallery that I was interested in, remembering what I liked every now and again and not thinking that my two-month-old infant needed another class.

I do know, though, of an AMAZING group, which began in my area and has now expanded into other towns, called 'Singing Mamas', which has a very different approach. Bring your bumps, babies, children (if you have them, no requirement) and sing together as adults. The babies and children are not the focus. You are. Your voice and your participation – the magic occurs when you realise that the babies, all around, are totally blissed out by the voices singing. They are content being around it. The women have something uplifting and special for themselves and the kids are perfectly, beautifully, held into the edges of that. All too frequently women share the 'losing' of themselves in the small baby months; allowing yourself to be the focus from time to time is vital. I love the image of the solar system here; you are the sun, and the children are in your orbit, benefitting from your warmth and held steady in your light. Do not make the mistake of always making them the sun; they need to be your little satellites where you can keep them safe and watch their journey around you, and you need to be there, happy, central and important, where you can shine.

Let Them Do Things For Themselves

Unless they truly cannot, of course . . . It's the routine exit-classroom-chuck-the-bag-at-mum-before-even-saying-hello and expecting it to be carried to the car by great big Year 6s and 7s that gets me. Keep an eye out at any primary school home time and you will spot this happening. I felt like a pack mule when my children tried to do it to me. It's much better for them to be in charge of their personal stuff, or at least, to ask you for help if they need it. You need to be respected (not feared in any way) but not treated as a dumping ground. The expectation that you will just pick up what they throw at you doesn't set a good behavioural dynamic between you for years to come. Putting in the expectation that they will look after their belongings and, of course, you can help if that's needed, sets up a healthy, boundaried future for both of you and helps them to grow into successfully independent humans step by little step.

Don't Suffer Constant Interruptions

Again, I'm not talking about important interventions, like if a wasp has just stung them and they are swelling up, struggling to gain your attention – and I am talking about children without neurodiversities to embrace – but I would routinely see parents constantly cutting off a sentence midway to answer a question that the child has just thrown in. It's not a bad thing to ask the kids to just wait until you've delivered the whole sentence to the other person. It teaches them that they are not always the MOST IMPORTANT THING EVER (I know, they are . . .) and there's a great gift in learning to respect that your parent also has things to say, and learning the conventions of conversation. You will of course be able to judge it well and not be dismissive of your child and their particular needs, but stopping your own conversations the moment they interject isn't supporting them in understanding how most communication works.

Stop Allowing Them to Make All the Decisions

This is really controversial, I know. And, of course, I know that children NEED opportunities to make choices and to express their desires and opinions. All healthy and good. But it's about balance and trying to avoid the problems caused when the children become the people who call all the shots in a household. I've seen examples where parents have ended up having to go to really elaborate ends to engineer a situation that appears to be the choice of the child (in one case an entire house sale and school move) rather than face any situation where it appeared that they were not always providing exactly what the child wanted. In the long run, it's not good for them, or for you.

Children will, pretty much always, push out to find the boundaries and if you're uncertain and wobbly about where yours lie, and you default to asking them what they want, they mostly won't know and principally, it's not actually what they seek. It's hard to feel safe with a parent who has no boundaries and who offers all options. You can see this problem when kids are presented with too much choice in everyday scenarios, such as a whole supermarket shelf of sweets to select from and they just don't know what to do, it overwhelms them, which upsets you, and what was meant to be a nice treat turns into something stressful. If you're able to go into that type of situation and support the child with clear boundaries, 'You can choose this one, or this one – which one would you like?' and if you stay calm and clear, they will be OK with that, comforted even, and you will be able to offer them the things that you are able to offer. The same goes for clothes, food you're cooking for supper, holidays, days out . . . It's hard for kids when they are given the crown – as much as they seem to want to call the shots, that's what you're for. You can introduce more and more choice as they grow and as you are happy to; just don't feel worried about being in charge of decisions – this doesn't make you an uncaring parent.

Be Intentional with Toys and Activities

My children started their lives wrapped in the felty wholesomeness of the Steiner School world – it's an education system slightly similar to some Scandinavian countries where the onset of 'formal' learning, decoding abstract concept (that is, reading and the use of mathematical symbols) is delayed until the age of seven. The idea is that play, rather than decoding, is the work of the small child and that being surrounded by natural materials is best for the growing brain. It's an independent school but as the children's dad was a PE teacher there for many years, they had staff places.

Some of the culture around early childhood that we took from their limited time in that beautiful setting was absolutely golden and will stay with me for ever. I admit, however, to being a bit bruised by what happened when we were no longer able to be a staff family and my kids were rapidly shown the door, but I will take some of the good bits and focus on those.

As Steiner parents, we were taught that the objects we have, in this case the toys, held qualities beyond the immediately obvious. I already knew the generally assumed basics that Barbie = highly questionable introduction to body positive messaging, and Toy Guns = I don't even need to say, but what I found a touch harder to grasp was that we were told that all toys come with some sort of a heritage, a soul, a backstory, a weight to them.

Something stamped out of a mould in a plastics injection factory in China, and shoved, along with tens of thousands of identical items, into a crate by an underpaid worker to be transported to a gargantuan warehouse and loaded into a delivery truck, will not, we were told, hold the same human connection and richness for our children as a simple doll or a ball sewn by hand and filled with the time and love of the person who actually enjoyed the process of creating it.

Don't cringe – bear with me. I, too, thought that this was just the indulgent propaganda of the wealthy leftie elite, but it became something I really believe in now, even with my limited budget and penchant for a bargain. You do start to feel that there is a different 'something' about those things that were made for your kids, or at the least, made more gently. I can't quite say that a doll, a toy boat or a ball has a soul, but I actually do now believe that they have something warmer in their very matter than the mass-produced stuff, and I do believe that there is a great benefit for children in reducing it all, in having enough. A 2017 study at the University of Toledo by Dr Alexia Metz concluded that for toddlers, the optimum number of toys in a playroom environment was just four.[1] When there were more, they were unable to settle and find a way to play without further distraction. With fewer options, the children were able to investigate a few things and to come back to the one that they found most engaging. They stayed with the chosen toy, really investigated it and all its possibilities, even managing to switch into imaginative play.

This study can help us to allay some of the fears around the quest to find the 'best' toys, the 'right' ones to stimulate and educate and set our children up for the best possible outcomes.

If you are going to take heed of the Toledo study and its findings, you'll probably want to reduce the number of toys that your child owns. I read quite an old study which had pulled data from official sources and used simple calculations to roughly estimate that the average British child owned 493 toys throughout the first 13 years of their lives, enough to fill 34 wheelie bins,[2] and I suspect the figure from over a decade ago will have been even higher, with the growth of online shopping.

With small children, I would suggest that a great way to help them to get the most from their toys and games would be to start rotating what they have access to so that there are fewer things available at any one time, and you can keep changing the offering. Pass things on as soon as your child outgrows them or loses interest. And see if there are opportunities to reduce the toys that are so specific, so fixed and finished that they can never be anything else. They can't be transferred. A motorbike in miniature detail can't be a truck, a buggy, a stone, The King of Wasps or a cake – it can only ever be a motorbike. A bag of large smooth stones is not only free, non-toxic and without profit, but it is able to become anything. As mentioned in Chapter 5, the brilliant educationalist, the late Sir Ken Robinson, pointed out that children are sadly taught 'out' of their imaginations, not 'into' them,[3] so your tiny ones won't dislike stones and pine cones; they will use them in a thousand ways that you can't even begin to imagine.

I totally recommend having a look at Waldorf kindergarten Pinterest ideas if you have small children and seeing if you can adopt some of the ideas you will see for creating enriching and exciting imaginative play opportunities for your children at very little cost. The ideas that you will see include building up play resources that are highly adaptable to the billion different scenarios that children will throw themselves into. They tend to include the staples of:

- a play frame (like an old wooden clothes horse) for hanging cloths / throws on and creating 'walls' to make a shop, a school, a house, a rocket, a ship – any imagined place at all

- small baskets of smooth stones (big enough not to be swallowed), pine cones, wood blocks, etc.

- little folded pieces of cloth to become beds, floors, rivers, hills, etc.

- wooden animals

- unformed / rounded basic wooden cars, etc.

- wooden pegs

- wax crayons (usually little blocks) and paper, ready to go.

If you have access to a carefully kept area or shelf with this type of simple 'toy' in reach of small children, they will be able to use these things as props to create fantastic worlds and to imagine their own stories and characters. My children had some of their most engaging and creative days of play with characters imagined from plant pots, shoes and spoons. They did not feel that they were missing out in any way. I would choose fewer, more meaningful things time and time again if I could go back and pull out what I thought was best for my small children.

As I mentioned right at the very start of this book, and again in Chapter 8 on holidays, a skill that seems to be slipping through our fingers and one that we would do really well to support our children with, is the skill of waiting. Our lives are so heavily supported by technology, machines, apps and logistics, which have been constructed in order to diminish the act of waiting for anything. What we are exposed to as young children will form an essential part of our characters. As Aristotle roughly decreed, 'Give me the child until they are seven, and I shall show you the adult' so if we try to actively build in the ability to wait for things, it will help a child to regulate their impulses and face waiting with much greater ease as an adult. You can do this in small ways, by having a paper calendar visible and ticking off days, marking on it any routine and any fun events coming up so that the children can see how they are moving steadily towards a goal. Marking festivals throughout the year and building traditions is a very important part of parenting; it establishes a deeply grounding rhythm of home.

THE IMPORTANCE OF LITTLE THINGS

It's quite magical how the most mundane and ordinary things, to us as adults, may be the things that in twenty or thirty years' time elicit feelings of great nostalgia and emotion in our children.

I have an egg-poaching pan, an old and well-used aluminium pan of the style that were incredibly popular in the sixties and seventies. This pan, filled with water and kitted out with its four little individual scoops used to sit on top of the old gas cooker in our family kitchen. I remember our dad slicing a triangle of butter into each scoop and cracking an egg into it. I remember the thrill of watching as the perfectly poached egg was turned upside down and tipped out onto the waiting slice of Marmite toast. We were a big family, but the egg poaching pan could do four at once, so you didn't have to wait long for your turn. It was a lovely supper and I loved it when I saw that pan sitting on the cooker, the water getting up to temperature.

I now have that pan in my kitchen cupboard and have taken a piece of my childhood into the present. I have something that means something. An egg pan. I can bet you my parents didn't set out with that as their idea of a legacy item for one of their children!

In sharing this, I hope I'm helping you to see that you do not need to create an Instagrammable nursery for your brand-new child; you don't need to have a house full of toys and every new distraction that Hamley's can offer. A great childhood comes from being loved and listened to, from doing things together, from sharing time with family and friends, and from the safety of the familiar, even if the familiar things seem inconsequential, over time those constants become the tethers for our hearts.

Task: The Precious Few

Think of a home from your childhood, a place where you spent time and felt safe. Think of an object from that home that you can visualise very well. Perhaps something that you used while you were there. Part of the tradition of that home. Place it in this special museum case and give it a label. Take a moment to honour it and to consider what you can do in your life to continue to create these meaningful relationships with fewer, better possessions.

Think about your home now. Can you predict what item

or feature that a child in your home would create a deep memory of? What is special in your house?

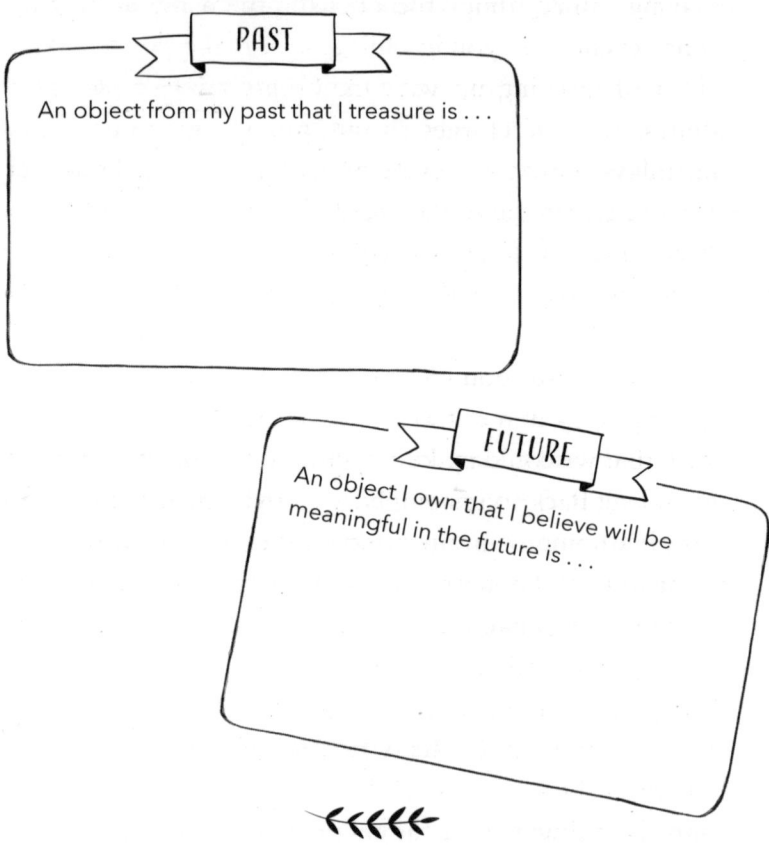

Sometimes the very simple things capture us in the deepest way. Not having everything new all the time leads to being creative with what you do have. Holding onto precious things creates traditions around them and traditions create grounding and stability. In not buying new, you'll be creating a strong anchor of memories for the people who witness you.

WHAT TO DO ABOUT PARTIES?

Having talked about the importance of celebrating seasonal events for young children, and the good, calming effect of growing up with the ability to wait for special things, we can't forget to talk about the importance of birthdays within the cycle of the year – to acknowledge the excitement and the madness associated with them. According to the very well-frequented internet source Netmums, the average UK parental spend on a child's birthday party is £524.[4]

What are we doing? This seems totally out of control. I'm going to make it very clear where I stand on this: I wish that we could make a collective agreement to rein this in and get back to uncompetitive, joyful little gatherings in people's homes. I am part of a generation who only ever went to birthday parties in people's houses, played games that involved chairs, balloons, paper donkey tails, shared some crisps and jelly, and took a slice of a homemade sponge cake home in a paper napkin. The guests brought round a little gift for the birthday person, the parents usually nipped off as soon as they had called a quick 'Hello!' into the hallway, and the whole thing lasted a few hours at the most.

There were no party bags filled with themed trinkets more expensive than the guests should even feel they have to bring for the birthday child. There were no personalised napkins, cups or balloon arches, no hiring out of entire restaurants, professional caterers, photoshoots, cake-smashes, mocktail menus, sushi platters and Prosecco for the adults, or timing and RSVP spreadsheets required (apparently not unknown in the build-up to these events).

There is so much stress built into the bizarre expectation that children's parties need to be like this now, and the only way that we can pull the beast back is by deciding that we won't be participating in the escalating action here and we will not succumb to shame for taking this stand. You have to take on the Teflon attitude to get through it if you want to reject it; do not let the fear of being 'the only one who isn't' stick.

When children are very small, they have no idea what's happening on their birthday and they would be totally oblivious to hundreds of pounds being spent 'for them' anyway; it's a way for the adults to celebrate their beloved baby and to show the people in their lives that they will spare no expense and stop at nothing in the quest to be the best parents that they can be. This is actually both natural and understandable. However, it's important to remember that being a wonderful parent is not assessed in any way by the money that you are able to spend on a single day, or whether you have coordinating tableware for a toddler's first birthday. The love and devotion that you have for your child will be acknowledged and noted in so many other ways than this, in your chats and songs, your delight at their little faces, your sleepless nights, your walks with the buggy to feed ducks, your trips to story sessions at the library. Believe me, you don't need to hire the Natural History Museum and a party planner for your love to be seen or felt, particularly not by your child and they are the only person you're aiming to impress with your love.

One of the greatest-ever pieces of parenting advice that I was treated to, and I remain eternally grateful for, was given by my child's nursery class teacher to the whole group of parents at an information evening in the school building. He told us that in his many years of experience with very young children and their parents, the most frequent feedback after all kinds of big birthday parties was that the birthday child had not enjoyed the event. Overcome with the occasion, all the fuss and change of routine, small children have a tendency to want to withdraw into safer, more familiar spaces and will often remove themselves from the party to be found upstairs, or outside, or anywhere away from the main activities. The teacher's brilliant advice to all of us assembled there, many of us totally new to parenting and living with under-fives who cannot possibly explain what they are truly thinking and processing, was that, as a general rule for birthday parties, the age that the child is becoming is a good benchmark for how many children should be at the celebration, including the birthday one. He specifically suggested not to invite the whole class. He gave us the green light to keep it small, and the understanding not to be offended if we were left out of some of the groups. If I could give every new parent a present, it would be the gift of that public chat, with their contemporaries also listening. It took the frenzy out of the parties for the next seven years for me – as a kindergarten teacher, he had my son from age three to seven, and then my daughter too, when she was old enough to join, and that one mic-drop bit of advice saved me from the pressure of the huge party.

**

As they grow, constant adapting will be required to enable you and your child to cope with the evolving pinch points of parenting. Just when you think things have settled and you've sorted out one set of conditions, there will be a change of dynamic and something new for you to manage. There are too many separate things to tell you here what you should and shouldn't do in order to manage a great relationship with your child throughout all the years and the different stages of 'want' that they will experience. Some of the wanting will be easy – it'll be things that you also admire, things that you are able to borrow and inherit, things that you consider to be investments in their future, but there will also be the 'grimace' items, the things that you wish they didn't want but have set their hearts on (iPhones, particular trainers, the current doll craze) and these are the things that you'll have to do some negotiating over. My advice would be to let some of the dreams come true, but not all. Make some things into special birthday presents, build waiting into the plan, and let some things go. Often the child will lose interest after a few weeks anyway and the thing that was driving them wild, and driving you apart, will slope off into the past with no further mention. If you are able to show that it's not always a no, and it's not always a yes, then you will be in good stead for a future of discussion and compromise.

Modelling is your greatest tool as a parent. If you want your children to feel content with less and to crave fewer new and unnecessary things, you will have to play the long game. You may not think that its working, but believe me, years into this part of life in the tiny flat with my teenagers, I can see glimpses of them already having an understanding that it isn't the stuff that we can buy that will make us 'better' or 'happier' grown-ups. They have had years of cheap days out, sandwiches in a van instead of restaurants and theme parks, they have camped in fields, had bikes from the tip, kept the same second-hand school uniform for years. They have waited for birthdays to have dinners out, and they have had the smallest home in all of their friendship groups. They have not had access to new stuff often. Of course, there have been moments of real conflict where they wished for something else and felt frustrated and angry by the limitations of our experience, but those flashes dissipate, the unconditional love stays, and if you can remain steady, and believe that all will be well, if you can allow them to feel frustrated with it at times without feeling that you have to immediately remedy everything and plug the short-term gaps, you will be giving them a foundation that will feel very safe to them.

Don't feel that you have to model artificial happiness constantly; you will always find that honesty is a better option, as long as you are not catastrophising and heaping the weight of an unknown fear that isn't yet here onto their little shoulders. It's all right to say that you are not going to buy this or that, and you can switch to focusing on something that you do have instead.

Last word before I leave you with some bullet-point top tips for Not Needing New with children – there's an accepted idea that teenagers are awful. This seemed to take root with the nineties comedy sketch featuring the character 'Kevin' undergoing an instantaneous transformation from joyful, effervescent twelve-year-old on the stroke of midnight of his thirteenth birthday, to an arm-swinging disgruntled arch of anger. Don't fall into the trap of a self-fulfilling prophecy with this. If younger children are constantly exposed to conversations where they hear their parents discussing how awful it's going to be, how much wine they're going to need, how they 'only have two good years left' and all the other 'jokes' around impeding teenage eras, there's a high chance that they will feel so undervalued and aware of how unsupportive that feels, they will kick out against those who constantly said they were going to kick. If you tell younger children that teenagers are wonderful and capable and it's an amazing time, then guess what? They really do tend to live up to that.

Ways to encourage Not Needing New with children:

- Build waiting into life, make it normal to wait for special things.

- Use charity shops early on for finding gifts – remove the stigma.

- Encourage considered regifting, where you find specific homes for things you no longer use.

- Do not say yes to everything they push for.

- Have days out without gift shops at the end.

- Make it normal to receive an 'experience gift' rather than a material item.

- Join a library early on and make it a regular habit to borrow and return.

- Model mending things. Simple sewing and fixing in the home.

- Look out for your local Repair Cafe meetings and use the service to fix the household items that you are unsure about doing yourself.

- Support school second-hand sales, bring-and-buy sales, etc.

- Make it the norm to take picnics / own food out on trips in reusable packaging, and remember cups for refills.

- Look in skips that you go past – just discuss what you see and if you could think of another way of using it.

- Enjoy making things together. Baking and crafting at home. Model that homemade things are good enough to give as gifts and when you receive gifts of the same nature, show that you value them.

A Final Note

Hopefully in these pages you've felt both a shift in your confidence as you realise the possibility of adopting these values and a growing excitement for this new mindset. It's my heartfelt wish that you'll be able to use some of the Not Needing New discussions and tasks to support small changes that will make you feel far more grounded in contentment with all that you already have, aware that it could well be enough, and more.

I hope that you found the reflection tasks helpful and that you can flick back through the book and remember what each exercise revealed to you about your relationship to stuff; look back at the things you were longing for when you first started reading this – are they still what you want? Have you been able to 'WAIT, Visualise' before you decide to buy new things? Are you more aware of satiation in relation to objects, and how to notice the feelings that it creates for you?

The hope for *Not Needing New* readers is that there will be enough encouragement here for you to break out of any negative spirals of spending on things that are neither making you feel better in the short term, nor tackling the massive waste problem that we face collectively in the long term.

A FINAL NOTE

'Want' is a psychological experience whereas 'need' is a physiological one, and as hard as it is (I'm not saying it's easy!), we can train ourselves to want fewer things, as long as we have all that we need. This is where the idea of the 'Joy of Enough' comes in; it's a sort of tagline that I've been using on social media to celebrate real and actual happiness forged through understanding that some of the most 'ordinary' parts of our lives are the places where we are extraordinarily lucky.

As soon as you have a surfeit, a glut, an oversupply of anything, human behaviour dictates that you will start to treat it poorly. Anything in abundance loses its value for us and we forget to treasure it. This is true not only of the things that nature has provided (think of how we treat weeds, think of what we do to our oceans and seas), but is true of the objects we have produced that we keep churning out, using once, and then burying or burning. How bizarre it is to think that we only have to spin the wheel of time back by 150 years, to imagine pre-industrialised glass manufacturing and how extraordinary it would seem to some of the furnace operators of that day to witness us using a perfect glass jar once, for one serving of one meal, before we toss it away to be melted down and made into another object. We have so many clothes on the Earth that there are beaches in countries all over the world where the gently rolling waves touch, not the white sands of the past, but a deeply clogged and tangled carpet of our waste – where we ship out our discarded textiles for another community to deal with and where thousands and thousands of tonnes of fast fashion break down in a briny graveyard.

If you can lessen your personal consumption, you will

be taking the most brilliantly effective steps to helping the Earth recover. You can be very proud of that.

But, of course, I don't wish you to do any of this work without happiness and joy at its heart! The difference between short-lived pleasures and a lasting happiness is really the solid legacy of Not Needing New that I hope you will take with you for the rest of your lives. You can throw all the money that you'll ever earn in the direction of pleasure – buying new things, dressing to the nines, having the most luxurious house on the block, jetting here and there and collecting gadgets – but real happiness will come to you via a different door.

I hope you have seen through some of the tasks in the book that your real happiness in life is found in your relationships, your memories, your safe spaces and your communities. You do not gain real happiness through buying stuff. You can be the richest person in the room and also the most unfulfilled and unhappy.

If stuff can't truly make us happy, if stuff weighs us down and producing so much of it creates environmental hazards; if stuff creates debt and fools us by making huge promises that it will never be able to fulfil; if stuff is not serving us as well as it should, it's time to stop investing in it.

We are capable of having fabulous lives with far fewer distractions. Notice the small things, be grateful for little things, delight in friends, family and everyday pleasures like walks, warm showers, good shoes, cuddling babies, watching birds, hot coffee, sunsets, cosy beds, freedom, music, and stillness.

I hope you can jump into your Not Needing New life

A FINAL NOTE

and feel happier once you're away from the pressure to have more and more, because honestly, despite what the ads tell you, it's lovely once you're in.

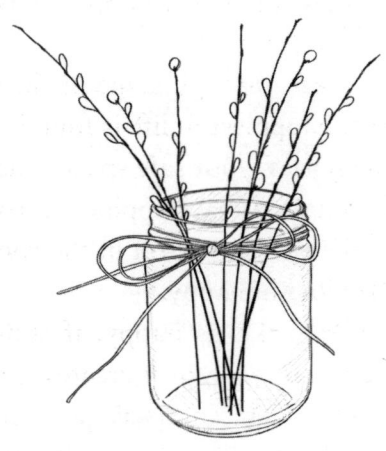

Recommended Resources

Here are some key inspirational accounts to help you on your Not Needing New journey:

Nancy Birtwhistle: @nancy.birtwhistle – an environmental focus to cleaning and inspiration on reusing common household objects.

Patrick Grant: @patrickgrantism – for his encouraging way of making it both elegant and mainstream to focus on creating a life with fewer, better intentionally selected items.

Amanda Lee McCarty: @clotheshorsepodcast – a brilliant account with extremely well researched and well-presented information on sustainability in terms of textiles and fashion.

Ellie Curshen: @ellypear – a well-known food writer and chef who brings a multitude of inspirational ideas around using leftovers and reducing food waste at home.

Oluwaseun Ogunsola: @the_oluwaseun – a London based styling editor for Selfridges who has been featured in *British Vogue* for her beautiful and original styling of preloved clothing.

RECOMMENDED RESOURCES

Kate Maguire: @convertedcloset – a Brit in New York City who is responsible for styling Sarah Jessica Parker and who consistently advocates for creating high fashion from reclaimed fabrics.

Erin Eggenburg: @wrenbirdmends – a Portland-based visible mender who shares a wealth of beautiful stitching techniques to keep textiles working.

The Seam: @theseam.uk – the UK's most trusted repair and tailoring service for clothes, shoes and bags – often showing the incredible possibilities of repair.

Damanjot Kaur: @did.i.see.plastic – a Punjab-based young environmental activist who shares passionate content around being a considerate, respectful user of the Earth's limited resources.

Community Repaint: @communityRePaint – the UK's paint-reuse network. A first-stop when thinking about decorating at home.

The Or Foundation: @theorispresent – a non-profit organisation advocating for justice in the fashion world.

Melanie Rickey: @theenoughness – a London-based journalist and style director at *Good Housekeeping UK*, who runs the podcast *The Enoughness*, based upon finding your 'just right' in life.

Caroline Jones: @knickers_models_own – a London-based stylist and charity shop volunteer who has undertaken two separate years of wearing totally preloved outfits every day for the full year. She shares brilliant styling hacks to elevate what you already own.

Acknowledgements

Firstly, my literary agent, Alice Lutyens, without whom there would be no book, only a vague fantasy about being a writer when I'm a grown up, whenever that will be. Alice popped into my Instagram DMs and asked me if I'd ever thought of writing a book. I had no idea who she was, or how fantastically lucky I was that she read one of my posts and saw something that she liked. Alice expects hard work, and I wasn't going to let her down. It took her a long time to shape me up, but here we are.

Jessica Duffy was the editor I chose from a little handful of publishers who met with me about my proposal; she was truly excited about what we could do with Not Needing New and I instantly felt that working with her would feel safe and supportive. I was right. It's been an incredible experience to witness the process of how a book becomes a real, published thing and to be guided through it all by these two lovely people and their teams.

I am grateful to Jules, who offerered that moment to step away from the classroom and, with it, the headspace to write. His morning chats have taught me so much, from Bernays to bicycles.

ACKNOWLEDGEMENTS

I want to say thanks to my wild and ridiculous tribe of siblings. Without them life would not feel anything like as enough as it does. We are a raft and we cling together.

Thanks to parents who showed us that massive tables with benches, minibuses, crab-fishing lines, bags of odd socks, old fruit machines in the playroom, egg sandwiches by the cold North Sea, jumble sale coats and walks to find cholera pits in churchyards were all the best bits of growing up. Fancy stuff can belong to anyone – magic is much harder to find.

Thanks to my children's dad and his beautiful new family who have shown us such acceptance and love. What broken families can look like after the pain. It's human kintsugi.

Isaac and Amalia – thank you for believing in your mum. You are glorious animals and you've coped with a lot. A LOT.

I am unbelievably proud of you.

And Aonghus. The quietest clever guy you'll find. He brought me peace, daal, four more little hearts to weave into my own, and the ability to really see what enough looks like.

There are people who pay him to build their extensions, without ever knowing that the dusty guy pulling out chimneys and sorting the underfloor heating holds the keys to the sweetest sort of happiness there is.

It's a good job you don't like writing, Gus, because a lot of this book is your work.

Notes

PART 1
Chapter 1: What Is Enough?
1   'Enough' definition. *Cambridge Dictionary*. Cambridge: Cambridge University Press, 2025. Available at: https://dictionary.cambridge.org/dictionary/english/enough [accessed 6 August 2025].

Chapter 2: Finding the Sweet Spot
1   'Financial Lives 2020 survey: the impact of coronavirus'. Financial Conduct Authority, 11 February 2021. Available at: https://www.fca.org.uk/publication/research/financial-lives-survey-2020.pdf [accessed 6 August 2025].
2   'The Money Statistics November 2024'. The Money Charity, 2024. Available at: https://themoneycharity.org.uk/money-statistics/november-2024/ [accessed 6 August 2025].

Chapter 4: The 'Do-I-Need-It?' Filter
1   'Global advertising spend to pass $1 trillion for the first time this year'. WARC, 26 November 2024. Available at: https://www.warc.com/content/feed/global-advertising-spend-to-pass-1-trillion-for-the-first-time-this-year/en-GB/10119 [accessed 6 August 2025].
2   Information on Edward Bernays and his marketing

campaigns compiled from various sources, including: 'Edward Bernays'. Wikipedia, 2025. Available at: https://en.wikipedia.org/wiki/Edward_Bernays; Jackson Carpenter, 'How Lucky Strike Became an Icon of the Feminist Movement'. Cultural Currents, 25 January 2023. Available at: https://www.culturalcurrents.institute/post/edward-bernays [all accessed 6 August 2025].

3   Sam Anderson, 'How many ads do we really see in a day? Spoiler: it's not 10,000'. The Drum, 3 May 2023. Available at: https://www.thedrum.com/news/2023/05/03/how-many-ads-do-we-really-see-day-spoiler-it-s-not-10000 [accessed 6 August 2025].

4   Abraham Maslow, 'A Theory of Human Motivation'. *Psychological Review*, 50(4), pp.370–96. American Psychological Association, 1943. https://doi.org/10.1037/h0054346.

5   'Sit Down' by James (Rough Trade). Lyrics by Gavan Michael Whelan, James Lawrence Gott, James Patrick Glennie and Timothy Booth © Kobalt Music Publishing Ltd./Universal Music Publishing Group, 1989.

Chapter 5: What to Get Rid of and How

1   '20 years of recycling progress'. Recycle Now and WRAP, 10 October 2023. Available at: https://www.recyclenow.com/news-and-campaigns/recycling-progress [accessed 6 August 2025].

2   William Morris, 'The Beauty of Life'. Lecture to the Birmingham Society of Arts and School of Design, 19 February 1880.

3   'Food Waste – 2025 Facts & Statistics'. Waste Managed, 2025. Available at: https://www.wastemanaged.co.uk/

our-news/food-waste/food-waste-facts-statistics/ [accessed 6 August 2025].

4   Josh Jackman, 'Food waste facts and statistics'. The Eco Experts, 12 April 2024. Available at: https://www.theecoexperts.co.uk/news/food-waste-facts-and-statistics [accessed 6 August 2025].

5   Sir Ken Robinson, 'Changing Education Paradigms'. RSA Animate (The Royal School of Arts), October 2010. Available at: https://www.ted.com/talks/sir_ken_robinson_changing_education_paradigms [accessed 6 August 2025].

PART 2
Chapter 6: Fashion v. Style

1   GlobalData figures quoted in Lauren Cochrane, 'Cheap, cool and kind to nature: how secondhand became UK fashion's main attraction'. *Guardian*, 12 February 2023. Available at: https://www.theguardian.com/fashion/2023/feb/12/secondhand-clothes-uk-fashion-cheap-cool-kind-to-nature [accessed 7 August 2025].

2   Evidence from the Textile Recycling Association cited in Environmental Audit Committee, 'Fixing fashion: clothing consumption and sustainability'. UK Parliament report, 19 February 2019. Available at: https://publications.parliament.uk/pa/cm201719/cmselect/cmenvaud/1952/full-report.html [accessed 7 August 2025].

3   UN Environment Programme, 'The environmental costs of fast fashion'. UN Environment Programme, 24 November 2022. Available at: https://www.unep.org/news-and-stories/story/environmental-costs-fast-fashion [accessed 7 August 2025].

4   UN Environment Programme, 'Putting the brakes on

fast fashion'. UN Environment Programme, 12 November 2018. Available at: https://www.unep.org/news-and-stories/story/putting-brakes-fast-fashion [accessed 7 August 2025].
5   Adela Cardona, 'Is Fast Fashion Overconsumption Bad for Your Happiness?'. Eco-Stylist, 20 December 2022. Available at: https://www.eco-stylist.com/is-fast-fashion-overconsumption-bad-for-your-happiness [accessed 7 August 2025].
6   Alice Murphy, 'Zara's latest sustainability effort feels like it's missing 500 points'. *Independent*, 22 October 2022. Available at: https://www.independent.co.uk/voices/zara-shein-second-hand-clothes-b2207995.html [accessed 7 August 2025].

Chapter 7: Health and Beauty

1   Grace Warn, 'Value of Beauty 2025: Beauty sector's GDP contribution outpaces UK economy but job growth set to slow in 2025'. British Beauty Council, 3 July 2025. Available at: https://britishbeautycouncil.com/value-of-beauty-2025/ [accessed 11 August 2025].
2   Tamara Davison, 'The Environmental Impact of the Beauty Industry'. CleanHub, 5 November 2024. Available at: https://blog.cleanhub.com/beauty-industry-environmental-impact [accessed 7 August 2024].
3   RÉDUIT survey results quoted in Ryan Morrison, 'Average British household uses 216 plastic haircare bottles a YEAR – and one in ten say they "can't be bothered" to be more eco-friendly'. *Daily Mail*, 20 August 2020. Available at: https://www.dailymail.co.uk/sciencetech/article-8647127/Average-British-household-used-216-plastic-haircare-bottles-YEAR.html [accessed 7 August].

NOTES

4   'Sporting and Outdoor Equipment Retailers in the UK – Market Size (2013–2031)'. IBISWorld statistics, 2025.
5   Gumtree Editorial Team, 'Turning Unused Fitness Equipment Into Cash'. Gumtree, 24 October 2023. Available at: https://www.gumtree.com/info/life/p/sports-leisure/lockdown-purchase-hangover-fitness-equipment/ [accessed 7 August 2025].

Chapter 10: Parenting with Enough

1   Cherie Spino, 'Fewer toys lead to richer play experiences, UT researchers find'. The University of Toledo, 18 December 2017. Available at: https://news.utoledo.edu/index.php/12_18_2017/fewer-toys-lead-to-richer-play-experiences-ut-researchers-find [accessed 7 August].
2   Plastic Box Shop Toy Ownership Research, 'Research reveals average child will own 493 toys'. Plastic Box Shop, DATE. Available at: https://www.plasticboxshop.co.uk/research-reveals-average-child-will-own-493-toys-i98 [accessed 7 August].
3   Sir Ken Robinson, 'Do Schools Kill Creativity?'. Talk at TED2006, February 2006. Available at: https://www.ted.com/talks/sir_ken_robinson_do_schools_kill_creativity/transcript [accessed 7 August].
4   Oxygen Activeplay survey results, cited in Alison Perry, 'With the average cost of a child's birthday party now £524, one mum shares how to keep the costs down'. Netmums, 1 October 2024. Available at: https://www.netmums.com/activities/with-the-average-cost-of-a-childs-birthday-party-now-524-one-mum-shares-how-to-keep-the-costs-down [accessed 7 August 2025].

RAISING READERS
Books Build Bright Futures

Dear Reader,

We'd love your attention for one more page to tell you about the crisis in children's reading, and what we can all do.

Studies have shown that reading for fun is the **single biggest predictor of a child's future life chances** – more than family circumstance, parents' educational background or income. It improves academic results, mental health, wealth, communication skills, ambition and happiness.[1]

The number of children reading for fun is in rapid decline. Young people have a lot of competition for their time. In 2024, 1 in 10 children and young people in the UK aged 5 to 18 did not own a single book at home.[2]

Hachette works extensively with schools, libraries and literacy charities, but here are some ways we can all raise more readers:

- Reading to children for just 10 minutes a day makes a difference
- Don't give up if children aren't regular readers – there will be books for them!
- Visit bookshops and libraries to get recommendations
- Encourage them to listen to audiobooks
- Support school libraries
- Give books as gifts

There's a lot more information about how to encourage children to read on our website: **www.RaisingReaders.co.uk**

Thank you for reading.

---

[1] OECD, '21st-Century Readers: Developing Literacy Skills in a Digital World', 2021, https://www.oecd.org/en/publications/21st-century-readers_a83d84cb-en.html

[2] National Literacy Trust, 'Book Ownership in 2024', November 2024, https://literacytrust.org.uk/research-services/research-reports/book-ownership-in-2024